Happiness is a Funny Thing

Written and illustrated by
Dave Caperton

Happiness is a Funny Thing
Copyright © 2009 by Alcus Media
Revised edition 2015

All rights reserved. No part of this book may be reproduced or transmitted in any form or by any means without written permission from the author.

Printed in USA

Special quantity discounts are available for bulk orders of this book for organizations. Special versions and excerpts can also be created for specific needs or groups. For details please contact:
URL: dave@davecaperton.com **phone:** 740-569-3859

For Suzanna

You are the love of my life, my companion, my inspiration, the mother of our amazing Alex and my best friend. Your reflection of God's light and love has touched every part of my life and has made it all beautiful. This "boo" is for you.

Table of Contents

Acknowledgements 9
Preface 11
Pursuing Happiness 13
A Why To Book 19
Changing Your World 23
The Gift of Humor 31
It's Just Gas 39
Don't Be a Rat 45
Everything is Personal... 51
Heigh-Ho, Heigh-Ho
(It's up to you, you know) 63
Humor as a Tool 69
Using What God Gave You 79
Elimination is the Key 89
A Gift to Give Yourself 107
Maintaining the Machinery 113
Playing with Pain 121
Writing on the Wall 133

Acknowledgements

The message of this book is not mine alone, but the result of many years of important lessons for living that I learned from the wonderful people I have been so blessed to have in my life. First, to the memory of my parents: my dad, who was bigger than life, but never too big to laugh at himself; and to my mom for her prayer, her love, her wit and her laughter. She was the first to teach me the language of joy. To my sisters, Sonja and Charmaine who are flawless examples of faith, love, compassion and joyful service to others. To my beautiful and talented son, Alex. He taught me more about happiness in the first day of his life than I could have learned in 100 years without him. He continues to inspire and amaze me every day.

Other individuals to whom I am indebted for their unique contributions to this project include: William J. Davis for his life-long friendship and his willingness to test that friendship by reading the first draft. Eric Gnezda for his encouragement and insights (and for all the breakfast meetings).

To the family members and dear friends I've loved who were with me when the journey began on this book and whose passing has since put these lessons to the test.

Finally, to my Suzanna, who is my chief encourager, my wisest critic, my true love and my best friend. With her in my life, happiness hasn't been hard to find. I just look beside me.

Preface

How many times have you heard someone start a sentence with, "One of these days I'm going to . . ." or, "If I could just find a way to . . ." These sentence starters are what gamblers call "tells." What they tell us is that we're not currently happy but we think we've identified what's standing in the way. So we set goals and work hard and perhaps actually get the dream job or the big house or the great body and then—like a desert mirage—we find ourselves no closer to the happiness we thought those things would deliver. What do we do then? We amend the goal and set our sights on a new point on the happiness horizon.

There are lots of books about how to get richer, fitter, smarter and better organized. At the heart of every one of those works is a single unspoken hope: "and then maybe you'll be happy." Books about personal growth rely on a sense of dissatisfaction with oneself; otherwise there would be no market for them. Rather than shooting all around the issue at the center of most self-help, goal-setting, moneymaking guides stuffing the bookstores, why not get to the happiness first? It may seem ridiculous to suggest that the flabby, broke, and disorganized could somehow experience joy without fixing all their flaws first. But why should that be?

Maybe we've been looking at this happiness pursuit from the wrong end all along. Perhaps your happiness has nothing to do with how perfect and profitable you are and all the striving to fix yourself first is really just an excuse to justify why you aren't happy yet. So, let's cheat. Let's forget about all the peripheral stuff and instead go straight for the prize.

Chapter 1
Pursuing Happiness

I am all for self-improvement: goal-setting, physical fitness, and all seven of the habits shared by the legendary effective people I've heard so much about. I simply think that a joyful person can learn just as well or better than a miserable person who think that slimming the waist and fattening the wallet are the keys to contentment. I say get happy first and then, if you still want to, lose the love handles and buy a Lexus. You'll probably be better positioned to accomplish those things in a default mode of joy than in a state of dissatisfaction anyway. Joy is a great motivator because when we're happy, we're energized and energy has to be applied somewhere. When we're happier we're more likely to do rather than to remain idle. Happiness is the fuel that can allow us to enjoy the now as well as provide a momentum to drive us to the future.

Like many abstract nouns—love, freedom, and justice— the concept of happiness is hard to define. We know that the founding fathers identified the pursuit of happiness as an inalienable human right, but they had the wisdom to stop short of defining it. It's an individual thing. What makes me happy is not the necessarily the same thing that makes you happy. Is it money? Is it love? Is it health? Is it faith? Well, yes and no.

In order to understand the concept of happiness and then make it a reality, you have to understand a little about how your brain works and how it deals with abstract concepts. The human brain is the most complex structure known. There are 100 billion brain cells in the cerebral cortex supported by nine times that many glial cells in the brain's white matter. These cells communicate with one another through thousands of connections called synapses along each cell. Each time a thought is launched or a memory is experienced, a certain synaptic firing pattern of neurons is triggered. These patterns, or networks, are the physiological basis of all thought and learning. The number of potential combinations of neural patterns represented by the billions of neurons in one human brain would be a number so large that it would dwarf the number of particles in the known universe. Now that's complex! Yet, for all its complex mysteries one thing is understood; it thinks in symbols.

When presented with an objective tangible idea (say a cocker spaniel eating dog food), the brain searches long-term memory to come up with sensory images to supply a visual representation for the words. Individual experience will influence details to a certain extent—the cocker spaniel I imagined has a black coat like my old dog, Casey, and is eating out of a red bowl like the one I use to feed my current dog, Topper—and that may not exactly match the image in the mind of the other person who thinks of a pug dog and a blue dish, but it's probably alike in enough basic details that we share more or less complete understanding.

When we're processing abstract concepts like happiness or love, things get more difficult. Now the brain doesn't have the objective symbols we can all agree on. There are cultural forces, familial influences, socioeconomic differences and on and on that will lead me to think about an abstract concept very differently than those who don't share the same influences. Happiness, therefore, may be symbolized in ways so disparate that we don't even come close to shared understanding. The MBA might think of symbols of financial achievement like a stock portfolio or an offshore account, the clergyman's symbols may represent matters of faith (or, depending on the clergyman, an offshore account), the young hip-hop artist might think of a lucrative recording contract and a tricked out Cadillac Escalade with 20-inch rims, and the new mom imagines future health and security for her child.

It's pointless to argue the merits of these symbols but it's important to remember that they're not happiness itself, just the symbols that the brain supplies to stand in for the real thing. Polish-American scientist and philosopher Alfred Korzybski observed that, "the map is not the territory". Many casualties have befallen intrepid wilderness adventurers who followed maps but lost sight of the fact that maps are static and unchanging symbols of dynamic and dangerous realities.

In our journey to find happiness we're all armed with maps crowded with symbols of happiness as defined by materialism, narcissism, selfishness, and envy. Those who draw the routes are ones who stand to benefit from our confusion, leading us to want to be richer, prettier, thinner, and more powerful but not an inch closer to joy. If we begin to regard these guides as reality we can end up with two equally undesirable potential outcomes:

    1. We fail to realize our goals.

    2. We achieve the prize and then realize that it's an empty victory that has wasted irreplaceable life.

I can't say objectively what happiness *is* but I can tell you for certain what it *isn't*. For one thing, it isn't pleasure. Pleasure is a brain event that can be stimulated by many things that are harmful to us and can destroy any real hope of happiness. Lab studies where rats were able to press a bar to stimulate electrodes embedded in the pleasure centers of their brains pushed the bar again and again until they starved to death beside a bowl full of food.

Generally speaking, the more effectively a drug works on the pleasure receptors in the brain, the more highly addictive and potentially destructive that substance is. Meth addicts know moments of pleasure so intense that they will throw away everything in their lives to experience it, but I doubt they know happiness any more than the bar-pressing rodent in the lab.

So it's not pleasure and it's probably not fame or money or the things that money can purchase. Don't misunderstand me. Money is something we all want. I like it myself, and although it may not buy happiness, the lack of it can cause a lot of unhappiness (the Great Depression described more than the state of the economy). Money can provide many comforts but, once acquired, the people who have it tend to become habituated to it. It's taken for granted like the air or the view of the ocean from their beach houses. A recent study concluded that for people who began below the poverty line, suddenly having $50,000 a year resulted in them reporting a significant increase in their levels of happiness. However, every additional rise over $50,000 resulted in less and less additional reported happiness with no measurable impact on happiness beyond $75,000. Researchers concluded that money could make a huge difference to our levels of happiness when it lifts us out of poverty, but succeeding increases do little to make us happier.

It's understandable that there is some confusion about that fleet-footed shadow called happiness that we all have the right to pursue. If you're stuck on a definition for your version of happiness, here's a good guide from a wise minister I once heard. He said, in order to be happy, you need three things:
1. Something to believe in (faith)
2. Something to look forward to (hope)
3. Someone to care about (love).

Money, health, and occupation can be useful vehicles to aid our pursuit, but when they become the goals themselves something sad happens. The very things that should help us to fulfill our purpose and realize our hopes become obstacles that destroy our faith, rob us of hope, and separate us from the people we love.

You probably remember hearing somewhere about the value of faith, hope and love and you're pretty sure I didn't originate it. You're right. But I'll make no apology for underscoring the truth that someone far more qualified than I came up with two millennia ago. I believe as Plato did that "learning is discovering what we already know."

I'll bet that there is a lot that you already know. You probably know how to eat for better health; how to exercise and get organized and save money; perhaps even how you could experience more joy and balance. Maybe learning *how* isn't what you need most. Maybe you need some *why*.

My wife and I own lots of cookbooks including some on baking that have very precise recipes that, when followed precisely, result in reliable versions of apple crisp or banana cream pie or chocolate cake. I've never been too concerned with precision in baking and therefore my results tend to vary from the picture in the book. Successful baking requires some science regarding ratios of liquid and fat to flour and heat to time. Within certain margins I can be creative and perhaps concoct an original dessert that surprises others almost as much it surprises me. If I stray too far from those ratios of ingredients and heat I end up with an indigestible lump of sugar that has to be chiseled out of the pan using methods known only to paleontologists. This is no cookbook for happiness. There is no step-by-step plan that will lead you to joy by the last page. Instead it's a book about the necessary ingredients and perhaps a little about the ratios. What you'll make with it is up to you. All I ask is that you read with a mind open to learn, a heart open to change, and a mouth open to laugh.

Chapter 2
A Why-to Book

Recently I was at a Barnes and Noble and I noticed what a large section of the store is dedicated to "how-to" books. In this section are the "Dummies", "Morons" and "Complete Idiot" series of books. Talk about feeling right at home. I think the success of these books makes some interesting and revealing statements about our culture. First, it underscores our expectation of immediate gratification taken to such an extreme that we have no patience for expertise to develop over long experience. Instead we want instant wisdom and knowledge about any subject that might be of interest to a large enough segment of the book-buying public. Today it's regarded as perfectly legitimate and reasonable to expect that expertise can and should be boiled down to one slim volume on any topic. By purchasing a book for less than twenty-five bucks I can supposedly learn how to buy stocks, build a web page, train a poodle, invest in real estate, sell on e-bay, or master twelve variations of poker and twelve steps to overcoming the resulting gambling addiction. Trying to fit every human pursuit into the same book formula has created some ironic and unintentionally hilarious titles. My personal favorite is, and I'm not making this up, **The Complete Idiot's Guide to Enhancing Self-Esteem.**

Another amazing revelation of the Dummies, Idiots, and Morons books is the apparent lack of shame we suffer about our own ignorance. I would balk at buying certain items at Walgreen's just because I don't want the checkout person making judgments about me even silently. Say I buy a certain ointment we'll just call the preparation even more advanced than Preparation "G". That's a confession of a problem that I might have (not really, I'm being hypothetical here for crying out loud). Now, say over in the food aisle they also have a great sale on canned refried beans and Tabasco Sauce and I toss that in my cart, too. I just know the cashier is going ring out the first item and then get to the canned goods and the condiments think, "Well, there's your trouble!" I don't need that. But let me go into a Barnes and Noble and I have no problem walking up to the young co-ed at the counter, plunking down my credit card for a book that says right on the cover that it's designed for the intellectually inferior. "I sure hope this has easy words because, as you can see by my selection, I'm an idiot."

You might think that brazenly insulting the intelligence of the intended buyer would be an impediment to the success of book sales, but guess again. The how-to information market is a billion-dollar-a-year industry including books, webinars, and e-books. The message is clear: we are dummies who need to know how to change. But the emphasis on how-to obscures the fact that for meaningful change to occur, discovering the how-to is not the most important step. The most critical question to answer is not how, but why.

When I'm leaving a building where I've just presented for a conference for healthcare professionals, I often have to walk through a blue haze surrounding the smokers gathered outside the exit doors. As a non-smoker it's always amazing to me that they seem so unconcerned with the hazards. Do they not know? It was in all the papers. Heck, it's right there on the side of the pack of Winston's. Yet, I've never once seen a smoker glance down at the warning label on the pack and shout, "Oh my *gosh*! Did you read this? These things are *dangerous*!'"

We can only assume that they know. So why do they do it? Sure, it's a tough habit to break, but so is breathing, so you'd think that given the choice . . . It couldn't be that they don't know *how* to stop. There are patches, gums, and pills to help, but the whole how-to stop smoking strategy is actually pretty simple—don't. Don't buy cigarettes and if you do, don't light them. There. If you needed a how-to on quitting smoking, that's it. You're welcome.

In truth, most people who smoke claim they'd like to stop but they can't or they don't know how. What they really mean is that they aren't sufficiently convinced of why they should. Oh sure, they know that smoking causes lung cancer, heart disease, emphysema, bad breath, tooth-loss, premature aging, blah, blah, blah. It's all so hypothetical, though. All those risks are so long term and I'll quit long before it does any real damage, and my uncle smoked until he died at 95 and he was never sick a day in his life, yadda yadda yadda. So all the how-to steps don't add up to change.

But then one day in the doctor's office they feel their turn to ice when he says that the spot in the chest x-ray looks kind of suspicious and he'd like them to get further tests. Maybe it turns out to be nothing serious, but if so, hopefully it's the why-to they've needed to find the resolve to do what they've known how to do for a long time.

You've seen people dramatically change their lives after a brush with death. Obese people skip the Twinkies, drop weight, and exercise with a dogged determination. Workaholic parents find time to take a family vacation. Type

A personalities somehow learn to quit sweating the small stuff. What happened? In each case there was a compelling why-to that finally overcame all the resistance to change. If the turning point that results in change were expressed as a formula, it might look like this:

$P=SQ > P=CH$

Where change occurs when the level of pain (P) associated with your status quo (SQ) finally becomes greater than the pain of undertaking a change of habit (CH). Of course it doesn't always work out that way. Sometimes the addiction or the habit is so ingrained that even the warning shot of a heart attack or the survival of a serious illness isn't enough to conquer a destructive behavior and the result is a life cut short. But for those who do make it back from the brink, who succeed in remaking their lives, they point to that critical moment when the change they once thought impossible was suddenly within their capacity to make.

A "turning point" is just another way of saying a why-to that is strong enough to effect change. My value as a writer and speaker is to try to supply a sufficient why-to to move people in the audience to change. The method I use is what your rhetoric teacher would have called *pathos* (an appeal to their emotions) and—using humor—I work to persuade people that they *should* change and while they're laughing, that they really *want* to change. The change I'm after is the simple but critical change in how they perceive and respond.

"Perception is reality" is the maxim that guides advertising campaigns trying to market everything from deodorant to presidential candidates. Ad agencies and PR firms spend and make millions every day figuring out how to alter perceptions of the buying and voting public. Far from passively experiencing the world around us, we choose responses that shape our world. That we actively create our experience is perhaps the most critical insight we have into understanding motivation.

Chapter 3
Changing Your World

Your mission is to change the world. How do you like that for a goal (at least no one can accuse me of aiming low)? Before you start to think you picked up a crackpot political manifesto (my first book, still unpublished), I should qualify that first sentence a little. I perhaps should have said I want you to change *your* world. In other words, I want you to change how you experience living and working in ways that will bring more joy, laughter, balance and success to your life.

It will be very simple. This changing of your world will result from acting on what you probably already know, perhaps even what you already believe. Your success will depend upon your willingness to commit to change (I said it would be simple, not easy).

Remember watching the 1939 classic **The Wizard of Oz**? It was a rite of childhood when I was a kid. In the days before video streaming, it was an annual network event every spring and it always got huge ratings. Our parents would plop us down in front of the tube to watch Dorothy's odyssey with the promise that we were going to love it. Then, for the next two hours small children would be traumatized with images of tornadoes ripping up houses, witches hurling balls of fire, helium-voiced munchkins and airborne apes dressed as bellhops. I didn't sleep for a week after I saw it for the first time. You know what creeped me out more than anything else? That mayor of Munchkin City. This tiny politician with his bizarre hair, his pointy ears and his curly shoes made the witch seem almost endearing by comparison. When Michael Bloomberg became the mayor of New York, I had a flashback.

At the end of the story, after all of poor Dorothy's crises and close shaves in the Land of Oz, Glenda the good witch appears in a pink bubble and tells Dorothy that she could have returned to Kansas at any time just by clicking her heels together and chanting, "There's no place like home." When Dorothy, clearly ticked, asks, "Why didn't you tell me?" Glenda trills, "Why, you wouldn't have believed me." At that point I don't think anyone would have blamed Dorothy if she had wrenched off the scarecrow's leg and beaten Glenda over the head with it. She wouldn't have believed her? I keep imagining Dorothy saying, "You mean I rode a tornado to a land with talking lions, scarecrows and tin-men seeking organ transplants and apple trees with anger management issues all while looking for a wizard and running for my life from a witch and her flying monkeys but the idea of footwear as a mode of transportation you don't tell me about because I might be too skeptical? And, oh, didn't I see you traveling by Hubba Bubba? Yo, Tin-man, let me see your axe for a second."

I won't wait till the end to tell you that you have had the power all along to change your life and your experience in ways that will bring more joy to every part of living. Our ruby slippers are perception choices and here's how you get to Kansas: It's not what happens to you that will determine the emotional quality of your life; it's instead how you choose to respond to it.

Experience is subjective. It's as unique as you are. Two people can do the same job with same people for the same number of years. They can share identical responsibilities and compensation and yet the contrast of their experiences will almost certainly be greater than what they'll describe as having had in common. The reason is that our experience isn't external but an internal response to what happens. My world is the result of my perceptions. It's not just what I see, touch, taste, hear, and feel, but the meaning I attach to all of those things. If I can understand what governs my responses to the external input, I can actively shape my experience. I can literally change my world.

What if you could change your world by choice? What would that mean to you? How would that power change your work, your relationships, and your faith? Could you see yourself becoming a more successful employee, or a better leader? How would it change your relationships? Could it make you a better mother or father, husband or wife?

Chances are you work in an organization that has an official mission statement. The mission statement is *de rigueur* in the business world today. It's also one of the most overcomplicated processes to come along in a generation of business trends. In case you're self-employed a mission statement is where you take a committee of maybe eight people and lock them in a room for a year. They in turn drink a Colombian mountain of coffee and go through a Brazilian rainforest of paper while they argue over whether "excellence" should be used twice in the same sentence and whether or not "impact" is a verb when you're not talking about wisdom teeth.

I always wonder what the rest of the organization is doing while they're in session? Are all the company members wringing their hands outside the door saying, "Don't you think we should do something?" "No! Are you kidding? We have no mission!"

Then one day the doors open and the committee emerges like Moses coming down from the mountain. "We have The Mission!" Heavenly music plays, fireworks explode in the background and someone says, "Let's put it on a mug!" And then they all go back to what they were doing in the first place.

Now I don't really think that a mission statement is a bad thing. On the contrary, I think a statement that succinctly declares what you aim to accomplish is a very good thing. Its greatest value is creating a focus for your efforts. So it's valuable, okay? I don't need mission statement committee members protesting outside my house (of course that probably won't happen. It would take them too long to decide what to write on the picket signs).

So every hospital, school, manufacturer, retailer, club, and hot dog vendor with more than one cart has a mission statement these days. Steven Covey advocates that even families develop a mission statement if they hope to be effective. (Our mission: To avoid killing one another at Thanksgiving…)

Steven Covey is of course the author and lecturer who gave us the **Seven Habits of Highly Effective People** phenomenon. He has been effective beyond his wildest dreams. Covey has built an empire out of his seven habits approach. You can now buy Seven Habits of Highly Effective almost anything including families, parents, teachers, and teams. I wouldn't be surprised if there were a Seven Habits of Highly Effective pets in the works (of course that's only one habit for highly effective dogs).

Covey's great accomplishment lies in how he has boiled down complex concepts into a few simple rules. Had he written a book with 426 habits, I doubt that it would have sold a dozen copies, but seven? Hey, even *I* can do seven. They include wonderfully simple concepts like his third habit about putting first-things-first. Of course I don't understand why first-things-first is number *three*, but then I haven't sold 100 million books so what do I know?

Sometimes I'll ask the audience if they're aware that their organization has a mission statement. All the hands go up. Then I'll ask, "Who can tell me what it says?" Most of the hands go back down. I don't do that to embarrass the people (although that is fun), but to point out that whether or not you know the words, you probably understand the mission and your role in carrying it out.

The core of every good mission statement can be boiled down to two questions: Whom do you *serve?* and how will you *succeed?* But I think we need a third part. That third element is a resolution: to *bring joy to the process.*

Is joy a worthwhile goal? If it seems trivial and selfish, ask yourself this question: Who would you say tends to be more successful, someone who loves what he or she does or someone who finds no joy in it? Oh sure there are people who are pretty good at what they do even though they don't enjoy it much, but might even those people increase their potential if they could derive more emotional fulfillment from their work?

If I enjoy what I do, it raises the chances that I'm going to better at it simply because it's going to help me to be more resilient, innovative and motivated. Of course it's not enough to just enjoy what you do. I may enjoy working with nuclear energy but if I haven't added training to my joy there is the danger of all my joy going up in a mushroom cloud. Still, your attitude about what you do is a good foundation for success because when you enjoy what you do you naturally want to get better at it, don't you? You want more knowledge and you want to improve your skills because it's part of your identity.

If loving what we do is so connected to being better at it, what gets in the way? What (or sometimes 'who') stops us from enjoying what we do? It might be change or conflicts, or the workload or any other source of personal stress.

Do you have stress? Most people admit they have stress. Some don't, but maybe that's because they're the ones supplying it. Whether or not you acknowledge you have stress, you do. We all do.

What is "stress"? The answer to this question is almost always a list of those things that cause stress like not enough time, too many deadlines, unrealistic goals so on. Those are stressors, but they aren't stress itself. Hans Selye, a Canadian doctor and researcher who was a pioneer in unlocking the mysteries of the stress response defined real stress. In the early 1950's he published his landmark book, **The Stress of Life** in which he defined stress as: "The body's *response* to any *demand* placed upon it."

You might be thinking, "Hey, wait a second. There are some demands placed upon me that I actually enjoy." That's true. There are things we do like running marathons or volunteering at a shelter that are undeniably demanding and yet enjoyable. Are those things stressful? Yes, but it's a good type of stress. It even has its own term. It is called, *eustress*. Eustress is the response we want. It is the juice of living.

All the books and talk of stress over the past several decades has created a mistaken conventional wisdom that stress is something invariably toxic that we should eliminate completely. You might think that being completely stress-free would be a wonderful thing, but be careful what you wish for. In physical human experience, a completely stress-free state has a name: dead.

As long as the body is alive and the mind is conscious, stress is a constant, but—depending on the nature of the stress—that isn't necessarily bad. The bad stress that we think of when we hear it discussed is more appropriately termed *distress*. Distress is when we experience a negative physical response to the stressor. We feel anxiety. We feel powerless and overwhelmed. In short, we perceive that we are not in control of our lives. The key difference between eustress and distress is our perception of control.

When you drive your car, you realize the demands of the traffic and road conditions represent risks. You know the risks are real. Yet except for bad weather driving or being stuck in a traffic jam when you're late for an appointment, you probably don't consider driving particularly stressful. That's because in most driving situations the driver trusts the soundness of his vehicle and his own knowledge and experience behind the wheel. You also expect that the other drivers will follow most of the rules. You know there are risks but you likely feel reasonably in control and so you can get from point A to point B without a session with a therapist.

We all have our own thresholds for what constitutes acceptable risks and consequently we can't say for certain that any specific experience will produce a eustress or distress response in a particular person. As a result of the individual nature of how we experience stress, we have skydivers and trapeze artists and Acapulco cliff divers but we also have people who hyperventilate on elevators. All we can say for certain is that our response to the demands of life is the determining factor of whether the stress you experience is positive or negative.

What is the key word in Selye's response-to-demands definition of stress? If you said 'demand' you may not feel in control of your life. After all, how much control do we have over the demands placed upon us? Well, probably more than we are willing to exercise. When your own manager tells you, "Here are the new sales goals for next quarter and you can see you're going to have to kick it up a notch," you could conceivably say, "Nah, I don't think I'll participate." You probably won't do that, but theoretically, you could. The reason why you probably won't is because you expect there will be a cost involved and that cost will likely be your job.

If, however, you want to keep on doing what you do, (i.e. remain employed or married or a parent) you're going to have to accept certain demands. But what about response? If the key to dealing with stress is the response, now how much choice do I have? Now I have more options, don't I? I can choose to be cynical or hopeful, flexible or rigid, angry or amused. What I need are some tools in my box of response choices.

Chapter 4
The Gift of Humor

You know, one day we're going to look back on this and laugh."

One of the most amazing abilities we have as human beings is humor. Human beings are different from most of the life on earth in that we have an incredible range of emotions. Emotions exist in other animal species but in humans the range is infinitely complex. But for all the complexity, the usefulness of most emotions is fairly simple to understand. Fear and anger are related to our physical survival by preparing us for conflict. Love serves our social and familial needs and ensures future generations. Grief and sorrow are testimony to the depth and richness of our connection to others. Humor, on the other hand, is still a puzzle for science. What is it for?

Some psychologists have theorized that laughter began as an expression of triumph over enemies. Kind of dark beginnings for something I do now while eating Oreos and watching the Cartoon Network. Although, it would explain a few things like why villains are always laughing. As a kid I remember thinking that being an arch-villain must be a hoot. These guys were always going "BWA-HA-HA-HA-HAH!" as they did their dirty work. Meanwhile Superman and Batman were always brooding about all the evil in the world and their terrible responsibilities in fighting against it. Consequently, they were the dullest guys at the office Christmas party.

Our Puritan ancestors presumed that goodness was equated with a somberness of character while frivolity was a sign of moral weakness. Maybe because of that, we still distrust humor. It is something that feels good and we seek out, but authority often fears it because humor needs a target and, as evidenced in the long and noble tradition of satire from Jonathon Swift to Jon Stewart, it has no respect for power or hypocrisy.

Humor is a tool with many applications and more and more, science is starting to take humor seriously. An entire field of research has emerged called gelatology (the study of laughter) and even the sober medical community is acknowledging that humor and laughter have therapeutic benefits for those suffering from pain and illness.

I once was part of an NBC affiliate news story on the healing power of humor. Patch Adams, the real-life doctor who was portrayed on the screen by Robin Williams, was also interviewed for the segment where he was asked by one of the reporters about research confirming the health benefits of humor. I expected Adams to enthusiastically cite the research that supported his unconventional approach to care, but instead he kind of sighed wearily and said, "Of course there is research that humor is good for you, but do we really need to have research to tell us that laughing is good for our health? I mean, has there ever been research to show any health benefits from being serious all the time?"

Adams went on to explain that he was exasperated because he believes that some things ought to simply be intuitive. We shouldn't need to have evidence of the hormonal and immune responses to joy before we make joy a part of the treatment. After all, he pointed out, do we need to be convinced that a hug has a specific therapeutic value before we give one to a child who is hurting? No, we just do it. Maybe we need a little more heart and a little less scientific analysis in the way we minister healing to others, and that's true for the apparently healthy as much as it is for the ailing. We all need to love, to touch, to embrace, to dance, and to laugh not because it is a way to forestall dying, but because it is how we should be living.

Over the last 40 years much information (and misinformation) has been published about the power of humor to improve health. For the most part, I agree with Dr. Adams. The benefits of some practices like touching or laughing or singing are so intuitively obvious to our spirit that formal research to measure their benefits seems unnecessary. Still, there is occasionally a study or a story that surfaces that provides compelling evidence that laughter is valuable for its ability to do us physical and emotional good.

The most famous case where laughter was credited as having a real impact on physical health was Norman Cousins. A journalist and tireless activist, Cousins was also the editor of the Saturday Review. He had already battled several grim medical diagnoses—including heart disease—when he was diagnosed with ankylosing spondylitis, a very painful degenerative disease of the spine. In his book about his ordeal, **Anatomy of an Illness** (1967), Cousins discussed how humor helped him to cope with pain and restore his health. He watched funny movies to make himself laugh and discovered that if he could enjoy even a few minutes of genuine laughter, he was able to enjoy several hours of pain-free sleep. It became part of his daily health regimen.

Although he wasn't a doctor, he had done serious research in the biochemistry of human emotions for the University of California's School of Medicine and he was onto something. More recent studies have borne out Cousin's observation that laughter is associated with the cessation of pain and improved immune response. He wrote books about his experiences and advocated for making a humor a part of a total approach to medical treatment until his death in 1990, over 25 years after his diagnosis.

Now, many medical experts agree that laughter is associated with the release of neurochemicals called endorphins that are more potent pain-relievers than any prescription pain-control substance on the market. Long-distance runners often report experiencing an endorphin rush (the "runners-high") where the pain of the punishing run is suddenly replaced by euphoria. Laughter likely produces a similar experience without having to jog 26 miles first.

Another healing benefit of laughter is the boost to the immune system after laughter. Some studies show higher levels of disease fighting "killer T-cells" and higher levels of immunoglobulin A in subjects who have just experienced laughter. Add to that the measured benefits of temporarily lowered blood pressure and improved circulation and respiration associated with laughter and we begin to see an image of laughter as not only life-enriching but therapeutic.

Years ago, the Harvard Medical School concluded and published a long-term study on the effects of personality characteristics on longevity. In this study, a large sample of men were chosen to be tracked over forty years to determine what possible factors might affect longevity besides genetics and environmental factors. One of the areas considered was personality. Assessments were made of the subjects' personalities and then evaluated to determine any correlations between those characteristics and longevity.

At the end of the study there were three characteristics that showed a strong correlation to exceptional longevity. In order they were:
1. A highly developed sense of humor
2. An attitude of service to others
3. Connection to others

So joy, purpose, and connectedness were traits shared by those who enjoyed long life. That's really not surprising, is it? Those are attitudes that are underscored again and again in philosophy and faith as being worthwhile. They are also those that are effective in coping with stress and change.

Although the study was done with only men, subsequent research has borne out the findings for both sexes. A great example that I ran across a few years ago involved a woman who was a case study of humor and longevity. Jeanne Louise Calment was a Frenchwoman who passed away in 1997. At 122, she was officially the oldest person in the world. Now I don't usually call people 'old'. I really believe that age is more a state of mind than of years. I've known youthful octogenarians and ancient 30 year-olds.

When I was approaching 50, I was bemoaning the fact to a friend who told me, "You know 50 is the new 30."

I said, "Can we do that?" It seems there would be some kind of law against that. Isn't it like a used car salesman rolling back the odometer on an '96 Buick Century? I'd love it if I could just lop off 20 years because some trendsetters decided it was ok, but wouldn't logic then dictate that 30 is the new 10? The Cub Scouts would be having Webelo den meetings with cash bars and giving out merit badges for retirement planning.

We do all sorts of things to deny we are the age we are. Men hold in their guts until they see fireflies, and they dye their hair with rinses that come in 24 shades but, oddly enough, not one that is associated with actual human hair. Women color, cream, and some even have their faces injected with bio-toxins and their lips pumped with collagen so that they look like something from the recycle bin at Madame Tussaud's.

I have to admit that lately the face that appears in the bathroom mirror surprises me. In the mornings especially I seem to be developing features that I can only describe as "Larry King-ish". What happened? Hair is not growing as well where I always liked it to and now sprouts in places it never grew before. And it happens overnight in a kind of Jack-and-the-Follicle-stalk phenomenon known only to middle-aged males. I'll find a hair clinging to my lapel and when I pick it off I'll find the other end is attached to my left earlobe. Is this natural? Is it hormonal? Is there a full moon? I don't know, but it didn't used to be this way.

I also make noises that I didn't used to make. When I was a young man I would hear old people grunting every time they got out of a chair or tied their shoes and I thought it was just something they did for attention. Then about eight years ago I dropped my keys and when I bent over to pick them up I involuntarily emitted a guttural, "urrggh." For a second or two I couldn't figure out where it came from. I turned around and said, "Dad?" but I was all alone.

They say that with modern medical care and breakthroughs in anti-aging techniques, the average lifespan could one day easily top 100 or even 150 years (what kind of noises will we make then?) for now though, 122 years old is pretty amazing.

By the time she was 110, Mrs. Calment's birthday was an international press event. Reporters from around the globe would descend on the small town of Aires where she had lived all her life. She would answer questions and recount the story of how she had once met Vincent Van Gogh when she was young.

Eventually, the interviewers would ask her to speculate on why she had lived so long. Certainly, genetics played a role. Her mother was in her mid eighties when she died and her father lived well into his nineties. But even with that favorable DNA, Jeanne had beaten the odds. More than once she offered laughter as a contributing factor.

"Always keep your smile," she said. "That's how I explain my long life. I think I will die laughing."

Perhaps that means that she was fortunate to live a long life of hilarity, free from serious problems, but I doubt it. She had outlived literally everyone she ever knew in her youth. She had lived through two world wars that decimated the population and caused enormous national suffering. She knew pain and loss and grief like few people ever could. Yet she also knew how to separate the really serious matters of living from the merely annoying.

Most of all, she knew not to take herself too seriously. When a reporter asked her at her 120th birthday what kind of future she saw for herself, she smiled and replied, "A very short one."

The greatest benefit of a sense of humor is its ability to keep us balanced and in control of our lives without taking ourselves so seriously that stress overwhelms us. It is more of an insulator than anything else, but that's no small thing.

My mother-in-law lives outside of Cleveland, but the place she really considers home is her native West Virginia. Every once in awhile when we're visiting, she'll treat us to one of her "hillbilly breakfasts". This breakfast consists of fried eggs, fried potatoes, fried bacon, and biscuits with gravy. I think the family crest is two skillets above a field of Lipitor capsules. Anyway, the skillets she uses are ancient heavy black iron and they were passed down from her own grandmother. Every time she uses them, the dishes she prepares are seasoned with the flavors of generations of family cooks. They are like holy relics that make cornbread.

Not long ago, my mother-in-law gave one of the skillets to my wife. Shortly thereafter I got up early one Saturday to attempt my own version of an authentic hillbilly breakfast. I spooned in a generous dollop of bacon grease and sliced up potatoes and onions while the grease liquefied in the heat of the pan. By the time I was ready to throw in my mixture of spuds and onions I saw thin ribbons of smoke curling up from the hot grease, a sure sign that the temperature was too high. I picked up the pan to move it off the burner and that's when I got a lesson in the excellent heat conduction properties of iron.

The skillet fell from my smoking fingers and clattered to the surface of the stove splashing hot bacon fat over everything within 10 feet and started a fire. I shrieked while I moonwalked in a puddle of hot grease while yanking open a drawer to find a potholder. Finally, I found one and wrapped it around the handle of the skillet and lifted it off the burner without further injury. After dousing the flames with a box of baking soda, I tended to the skillet-handle-shaped brand on the palm of my hand and began to chuckle at the slapstick scene I'd just played. At that moment, I looked down at the potholder and it occurred to me. That's humor. That's how it works. Humor doesn't make our problems go away just as the potholder didn't cool the skillet handle. They both just provide an insulator that allows us to handle what otherwise is too painful to come in direct contact with. And most of the time, that's enough.

Chapter 5
It's Just Gas!

A few years ago I had an opportunity to work with a group of cancer survivors and their families through a hospital in my hometown. I received a call from a nurse at that facility who asked me to be a part of their "We-Can Weekend" retreat. It was to take place in the early spring at a state park lodge. I gladly accepted the date, but as the weekend approached I started to get nervous. These weren't people dealing with the stress of job changes or budget cuts. These were people facing nothing less than life and death. Although I never doubted that humor could be an important coping tool for them, I did wonder if they would accept that from me. After all, I wasn't a doctor or a fellow survivor.

Finally, the day arrived and I watched the people filing into the big meeting room. Between the survivors, their families, and the staff there were maybe 200 people there. The room was long and rectangular with the podium at the far end and the doors opposite. Suddenly I noticed a young woman walking through the doors. She was an attractive woman, but not like a fashion model or a movie star. There was just something magnetic about her. She had a quality that drew others to her. If I had to name that quality the closest I could come would be "joy". She was well known by the people there. She even had a little group of disciples who followed her in and clustered around her smiling and laughing.

What was clear was that she was a survivor, but not only a survivor. She was going through the experience right then. Many of the survivors present had long since finished their treatments and were indistinguishable from those who had never battled cancer. This woman was clearly currently in treatment. She was pale and had her head wrapped in a scarf to hide the loss of her hair. But instead of brooding and focusing on her own problems, she was laughing and smiling and talking to the others around her and they too were smiling.

She also was wearing a tee shirt with something printed on it, which I couldn't see from where I was in the front of the room but she was one of those people who come right down front to sit without even being asked (I love those people). When she got close enough, I read her shirt. It said: "Hair by Chemo."

I laughed. And then, realizing that I was laughing at a cancer joke, I stopped. It was kind of like, "HA-HA-HA—*hey wait a minute.*" I stopped because, let's face it, cancer is not funny. On the top ten lists of things that aren't funny, cancer has to be in the top three (with the other two being heart attacks and prop comics). I thought later if there were any families not associated with the retreat who saw her coming down the hall, I'll bet a few of them were a little disturbed thinking, "How can she make light of having cancer?"

But she understood something that right then I didn't, which was that even in that experience where there were clearly life and death issues, there were also parts that were *not* life and death. The hair loss was not life and death. It was a temporary side effect of the chemotherapy. It might be inconvenient and embarrassing for her, and initially jarring for others, but it wasn't permanent. Her hair could grow back. So, she chose humor as a way of coping with that part of the cancer experience.

That choice gave her a handle of control over her challenges. It was a way of saying she wasn't going to regard her illness with any reverence or dread. On the contrary, she was showing her willingness to fight through her humor.

I was so impressed by that experience that I shared the story of that woman with other groups. A year later I was invited back to speak for the nursing staff of the same hospital and I shared what I'd witnessed the year before at their retreat. Afterward, one of the nurses told me that the name of the woman was Barbara. She also told me that Barbara had been in remission for 11 months and that she was doing great, adding that the nurses and doctors all agreed that her success was as much due to her attitude as it was to the treatments she'd received.

I shared the story of Barbara with others in many different industries and organizations. I remember one time in particular when the story of Barbara was helpful. I was speaking for our state gas association for their annual conference (now there are some fun people). This was right at the time when our state legislature was writing legislation that was going to directly affect the energy industry. Naturally, the members of the association were anxious about the fallout from the coming changes. Because of that, the conference promised to be tense. To help relieve that tension the planner thought that some humor might help defuse anxieties. As a result I was invited to provide some laughter to kick off the day on an up note.

As the meeting began, the planner greeted everyone and read over the agenda for the day. As soon as he mentioned the legislative issues hands went up all over the room. They didn't want to wait. They wanted to talk about what the coming changes would mean to them and they wanted to talk about it now. There were so many questions that the host made a quick alteration in the schedule and invited an attorney to shed some light on the language of the pending legislation. "Good," I thought, "maybe he'll alleviate some of their fears and they'll be more in the frame of mind to laugh."

The man strode to the lectern and fixed them all with a lawyerly glare over his half glasses. "Ladies and gentlemen, " he intoned, "I've read the language and I have to say, it's the end of the world as we know it!"

I could see the headlines, "Lawmakers Pass Gas Bill". Apparently, the association members could see it too because an amazing transformation took place. I watched a roomful of professional people suddenly morph into a Jerry Springer audience. People shouted and stood up. Spit flew everywhere. Then the host rushed to the front of the room and bellowed, "Time OUT!" like a referee.

"Folks," he implored, "I know this is stressful and complicated, but we need to have some order here and we need to get back on schedule. I promise that all of your questions will be answered at the appropriate time, but that's not now. We're fifteen minutes behind schedule and we have to get back on track. So," he continued, "without further ado, here's the humor portion of our program . . ."

I stood up and looked at all those faces, many still red and sweating. They exchanged looks with one another and some of them even mouthed "*humor?*" I imagine it's the kind of reaction you'd get if you gave a nudist a tie.

I began by telling the story of Barbara and it wasn't hard to read their minds as they thought, "What has this got to do with me?" When I finished I said, "Ladies and gentlemen I don't mean to minimize what you do or your anxiety about the changes you might have to deal with. I realize that it's a stressful time, but," I continued, "let's never lose sight of the fact—*it's just gas!*" Absolute silence.

It didn't earn a big laugh but that didn't make it less true. Far from being life and death, most of the matters that rob us of joy and create terrible stress and worry are really just gas pains: uncomfortable and painful but not life-threatening.

I would go on to tell you how humor helps to relieve the pressure but there is such a thing as carrying an analogy too far. Suffice to say that humor can be an outlet for many of the minor discomforts brought on by change, stress and the occasional burrito.

There was another chapter in the Barbara story. About five years after that first survivor's retreat, the nursing director for the cancer institute called me again. This time they asked me to be the honorary chairperson for their annual tree-lighting ceremony at Christmas.

I said, "Honorary chairperson, that's sounds important. What do I do?"

"Really nothing," she told me.

"Great," I said. "Sounds like a perfect match for my skill set."

"You just share whatever you feel might be appropriate for about five minutes at the ceremony, flip the switch and then we all go inside for refreshments."

At the event everyone gathered outdoors in the frosty December air. The tree was strung with white and blue lights. Each light represented either a current patient or the memory of someone who had passed on. I shared the story of Barbara and then my son, Alex, who was still small at the time, hit the switch and everyone applauded and hurried back inside for hot chocolate and cookies.

One young woman stayed behind. She told me how much she enjoyed the story. I told her, "You know, that experience has helped me get some perspective in my own life and I know it has helped other people."

"Well," she laughed, "the reason I enjoyed hearing it is because I AM Barbara."

It was true although I never would have recognized her. This was a beautiful young woman who looked the picture of health and she had a head of thick blond hair.

"I've been in remission for five years now," she said. "I'm a cancer patient, but I get up every day and I have to make a choice." She explained how she tried to keep her sense of humor and her sense of gratitude for her doctors and nurses, her family and her friends and mostly for God's blessing of every moment of life that before her illness she had taken for granted. She even admitted, "Sometimes I don't make the right choice, but mostly I do and I think that's why I'm still here."

We have that same choice and the good news is that what usually is challenging most of us isn't even life and death. It's just gas.

Chapter 6
Don't Be a Rat

O
ccasionally people want to know how I began my career in speaking. Sometimes they come right out and tell me how they'd like to do what I do. I don't blame them. It is a great job. You get to have fun with people, there's no heavy lifting and often free food. I remember once a man asked me for any pointers I might have for someone who wanted to become a professional speaker. I said, "There is one thing that's very important." The man leaned forward on his chair ready to catch the nugget of wisdom about to be bestowed on him. "You have to develop a love, no a *passion* . . ." (The man was now almost off his chair with anticipation of the secret to speaking success) "for chicken!"

There are other perks to the job besides free meals, though. At the top of the list is getting the chance to work with amazing individuals and organizations. Some years ago I was working with an organization sells lingerie via a famous catalog that really isn't much of a secret. Their headquarters are in central Ohio and it was, quite frankly, a good gig. The most challenging part was that they have giant blowups from their catalog on every wall of their facility and I kept losing my train of thought. I kept thinking, "Wow. When I was 15, this is exactly how I wanted to do my bedroom."

The HR director there had developed a yearlong in-depth management program. It would be a four-phase approach and it would give the participants all the tools they needed to be successful managers so he asked me to provide some seminars on coping with stress and creating what he called "career and life balance." He asked me if I thought I could give them what they were looking for. "Yes," I said, "but is it alright if I don't use that term, 'career and life balance'." I explained that I don't like the term because it implies that somehow they're separate things.

We've all the heard the term "career and life balance" but what does it mean? Do we have career on one side and life on the other? On Monday morning do you have to stop *living* so you can go to *work*? I know it feels that way sometimes, but that's really not the way it works (usually you have to be at work several hours before all vital signs cease). It's all life! Your career, your family, your time at work as well as the commute, are *all* life. My challenge and yours is to bring balance and joy to the whole thing. If we don't, we risk burnout.

Burnout, of course, is the end of all joy and consequently the end of all effectiveness. When you've been out of balance long enough you stop all forward progress in your life and you just try to outlast the pain.

There was a behavioral experiment I read about a few years ago that demonstrated this phenomenon called burnout with rats. In this experiment the researchers took rats and put them in cages. Now, let me stop here for a moment and say that, first of all, I'm sure that there is some legitimate research involving lab animals. That said, I have to admit that I feel a little sorry for the rats in some of these studies. They make them drink the rodent equivalent of gallons of diet soda or alcohol every day. They make them chain smoke one cigarette after another. Maybe they learn things but if they threw in ESPN, they could spare the rats and just do this research at the house of a guy down the street from me.

In this particular experiment the researchers put a group of rats in two separate cages with floors that were electrified to deliver painful but non-lethal shocks. At the touch of a button, the researchers would send that current through the floors of the cages. At intervals over the course of several weeks, researchers would push the button to deliver a brief shock to both cages.

What do you think the rats did? Turn on one another? Learn to levitate? Unionize?

The rats in cage 1 eventually did . . . nothing. They stopped eating. They stopped grooming. They stopped reacting at all. They just walked around going, (zzZAP!) *"That's just life in the cage . . . (ZZIZZ!) yeah, that's j-j-just the way it is and . . . (ZZZT!) there ain't n-nothing you can d-d-d-do about it!"*

What the rats in the first cage learned was helplessness. The shocks continued no matter what they did, so they finally just stopped wasting energy by reacting at all. They accepted that they were not in control no matter what they tried, so they just gave up. They burned out.

The rats in the second cage were a different story. Although they initially had an identical response to the shocks, they soon began to thrive in spite of them. What was the difference? In the second cage, the researchers had installed a bar. And because they could drink...wait, no, that's wrong. The bar they installed when pressed shut off the current. So, as soon as the current began, one of the rats would press the bar and turn it off. So, they literally had a handle of control that made all the difference. But here's the amazing part: that bar shut off the current to *both* cages. The rats that deteriorated and learned helplessness weren't subjected to any more stress than the rats with the bar to turn it off. The difference was that one group had no idea why it started or why it stopped and the other had a device that allowed them some perception of control.

Perception is truly reality. How you choose to respond can amount to installing a handle of control for your stress.

Your response choices are the determining factor of whether you learn helplessness or what happiness researcher Martin Seligman calls "learned hardiness."

How do you choose to respond to the shock of stress and change in your life? If you see no control, welcome to the cage. If you decide you have some control (even if all you have for coping is what Barbara had—a defiant sense of humor—you can create joy in the now even if now is less than ideal.

I remember once a few years back when I was at a restaurant having dinner and I noticed there was group celebrating the retirement of one their party. I gathered from the conversation of the people there that it was the retirement of a postal carrier. I had an opportunity to speak with the guest of honor later in the evening and I asked him how many years he had been delivering mail.

"Twenty-eight years," he said.

"Wow," I said. I'll bet it feels strange after 28 years, tomorrow there's no mail to deliver. Are you going to miss it?"

The man, whose friends had been buying him drinks all evening, looked at me stonily and said with a slight slur, but no hint in his voice that he was joking, "I have hated every *minute* of every *day* of it!"

I was shocked, and to tell the truth I was skeptical, too. I mean, come on, there had to be one good sixty-second interval sometime in 28 years. Somewhere on his route didn't he find a quarter or something? Let's just say, though, that he was telling the truth, at least for the most part. What he was saying was that for 28 years, maybe eight or nine hours each day, five days each week, maybe fifty weeks each year, he hated his *life!* That's what it comes down to, doesn't it? After all, it's all life.

I had to ask him why he kept doing it for so long. Without missing a beat he shot back, "Oh, the *benefits.*"

The benefits? What kind of benefits would be so great that they're worth sacrificing happiness for almost half of one's waking life? Isn't there something seriously wrong here? This man virtually traded away the best years of his life for a pension and a dental plan. What an appalling waste of life!

Those benefits that he added to each year by doing something he hated became the very walls and bars of his cage. He hated carrying the mail, but because he had so much of his life invested in it, it became unthinkable to leave it even though it caused him pain every minute of every day. Instead, he just absorbed the shocks like a rat in a cage until retirement would finally open the door and he could stumble out with his pension. That poor dumb rat.

What happens to the rat when he or she has survived the imprisonment and made it to the release date? In too many cases they just keel over. They hate their lives for years but they keep going, just counting down the days until they've completed their sentence and they can finally leave. The day finally comes and the door opens and they run out and say, "I'M FREE . . .(thud!)" Their entire purpose in living has been about surviving their term in the cage. All of their energy has been invested in that pursuit. But that level of distress is extremely high and requires tremendous life energy and when that supply is depleted and the goal of surviving the cage has been accomplished, there's often little else to keep them going and within two years of retirement, a significant percentage of these unfortunate individuals appear in the obituary section of their local papers with "retired from the Acme Rat Cage Corp." printed right after the list of relatives by whom they're survived. It's tragic and made all the more so because it doesn't have to be this way.

Chapter 7
Everything is Personal

"Would it help if I told you that this is strictly business?"

Have you ever had a really bad day at work? I mean one of those days when you just seem to have no patience for anybody? The punchline is, "Yes, it's called Monday through Friday!"

Sometimes we can't explain why we have a miserable day. Maybe it's hormonal cycles or maybe you are a little short of sleep or the milk on your cereal was sour or maybe the moon was in the seventh house but Jupiter just refused to align with Mars. Sometimes that's the way it is.

Most of the time, though, we can point to something specific that has so knocked us out of balance that everything is wrong. A fight with your husband or wife, a child who is sick and you can't stop worrying, you've bounced a check, the house payment is due and you heard a funny and expensive sounding noise coming from the engine on the way to work.

Whatever the reason, you're having trouble coping with the pressures of the job because pressures outside the job keep getting in the way. Maybe a helpful boss has pointed out that you need to "Leave your personal life outside the door!" Of course you'd love to, but there's a problem: It's all personal. Instead of leaving your "personal" problems behind, they just become filters through which all the work-related problems have to pass.

The frozen computer screen you took in stride yesterday makes you sob in frustration on the same day you learn the furnace is finally beyond repair. Because everything that happens to us is personal, all of our problems from relationships to corporate reorganizations become personal problems and stresses.

When we make artificial distinctions like personal/professional or career/life, we mislead ourselves that we should ideally be able to compartmentalize living. We talk about the stresses in our lives as if they can be neatly stacked and partitioned like Martha Stewart's walk-in closet. "Here are my personal relationships folded right next to my pastel cowl-necks, and over here are my emotional stresses alphabetized and ordered right by my earth-tone wool dickies." It's not so. Your personal and professional stresses and the mental-emotional-physical responses to them are more like the junk drawer or that suff-it-in-and-close-the-door-before-something-falls-and-gives-you-a-concussion closet that most of us have somewhere in the house.

Everything is personal. Every stress is a physical, a mental, and an emotional experience. That means that whatever happens in one part of us affects every other part.

When you have that awful, terrible, no-good day and you get home, do you leave it all behind now ready to be a great mom, dad, wife or husband? Or do you come home to your poor unsuspecting family and mentally superimpose crosshairs on each of their beloved heads? Admit it, we all occasionally take out our frustrations on our families and those closest to us. We vent where we feel most secure, where the love is the most unconditional. On the other hand, we take the pressures and frustrations from our home to work with us and that affects everything we do there. You might be patient and long-suffering by nature, but sometimes a stress or conflict somewhere else in your life will just lop off about nine tenths of your normally not-so-short fuse.

Instead of a clean separation between personal and professional, there's a spectrum of experience from the superficially to the deeply personal. Everything that happens in our life is connected to everything else.

Years ago I got a great lesson in how interconnected every part of life really is and also a good lesson on how we respond to change. It was when my wife and I discovered we were about to have a baby. Ok, ok, my wife was going to actually *have* the baby, but I helped. My wife was simply the one who had to face, you know, the risks and pain.

If you're a mother, you know what I mean. Having a baby is an amazing process in its complexity and risks. It's astounding that any woman does it willingly. Imagine if you had to literally buy into the idea of childbirth. If you sat down with a salesperson who gave you the pitch for motherhood:

"Ok, here's the plan. Over the next nine months you're going to double in size. During that time you're going to experience chronic discomfort followed by an acute agony and then you won't sleep for at least two years. Just sign there and we'll get things rolling."

I don't know about you, but I would be asking, "What other packages do you have? That doesn't really fit our needs."

Would there ever be a population crisis if that were the arrangement? You'd have to offer rebates and dealer incentives just to make enough people to staff the DMV.

Anyway, when we learned that parenthood was in our future it was just about the time we'd concluded that it wasn't. We had been married for eight years and our lives were pretty well ordered. We knew how much money we could count on in the bank each month. We knew how much free time we could count on. We also had lots of friends who were parents already who would watch us playing with their kids and then would say, "You two ought to have a baby."

I was just dumb enough to be flattered by this. I thought they merely recognized great dad qualities in me. I didn't know that they were really vampires trying to get us to join their colony.

So when the tests came back positive I knew those friends would want to share in our joy. When I told them, they were happy, but their response wasn't exactly what I'd imagined. They all kind of rubbed their hands together and smiled craftily saying things like, "Well, everything is going to *change* now!" I think what they wanted to add was, "Now you vill join ze children uf ze night!"

Things were going to change? I knew that. What I didn't know was the nature of change and how we respond to it. When we know a change is coming and we have some time to prepare for it, we usually experience it in two phases. First we try to reason with the change. We tell ourselves, "I'll make this adjustment and that alteration and I'll be fine." Soon, though, the emotional realization comes and when that happens, reason has nothing to do with it. It's hard to control the emotions. They're slippery. Sometimes the emotional awakening happens gradually as the change gets nearer. Other times it's all at once as it was for me in this experience.

Everyone is different and I'm sure my wife, Suzanna, had accepted the baby as an emotional reality long before I did. For me, the moment when my emotions woke up to the reality of parenthood happened when we went into the doctor's office for the ultrasound. If you have been through that, you know how exciting it is. Medical science has devised a way to see the baby before it's born, like a sneak preview.

When the doctor mentioned scheduling the ultrasound I asked him if it might reveal whether we were having a boy or a girl. "It depends on the position of the fetus at that moment, but yes, it's very possible," he said.

"Oh, I want to be here for that, " I told my wife.

We set up the appointment for the following week and all that week I told everyone I knew, "We're going to see the baby." I was very excited. When we got to the doctor's office I had no idea what to expect but it was clear that I was more amped up than my wife. I paced and fidgeted and thumbed distractedly through back issues of Babytalk magazine. Finally, the doctor came in and as he washed his hands, he said, "Ok, if you'd just lie down on the table," and then turned toward us and added, "I meant your *wife*." Like I said, I was very excited.

Then a nurse wheeled a cart into the room. On top of the cart was what looked like a little television with extra knobs and a small screen about four inches wide. Connected to the set was a long black cord that ended in a large microphone-like device. A nurse then rubbed what looked like mint jelly on Suzanna's belly ("that's the conductant," she explained), and then began to run the microphone over the area.

Up on the screen something began to happen. Grainy black and white images began to form and move around with the motion of the microphone. It was a little disappointing. This was the cutting edge of medical technology? A black and white portable with a four-inch screen? Frankly, I was expecting more. I was thinking more along the lines of a 50-inch HD and maybe a joystick so I could make the kid run, jump, and climb. Instead, here I was squinting at flickers of light on a black and white portable TV.

Just then the doctor turned around to me and said, "See the baby?" Well, I *wanted* to. That's why I came, after all. I was trying. And I was apparently the only person in the room who couldn't. All the nurses and my wife were gazing at the little monitor going, "Awwww." I was smiling and exclaiming right along with them because I didn't want them to know that I couldn't see the baby, but meanwhile I was thinking, "That's Doppler radar! This guy has pulled in the Weather Channel by mistake."

    The doctor gave us a printout of the image and I kept it with me. All the next week people would come up to me and say, "Well, is it a boy or a girl?" I'd take out the picture and say, "I think it's a cold front."

    Of course the doctor tried to show me what my untrained eyes were missing. He held the photo and said, "Do you see this cloudy ridge running diagonally through the picture?" I told him I could. "Well," he said, "that's the spine."

"Oh," I said, "yes, the spine!"

"And," he continued, "this round misty area at the end of the spine is his head, and the area at the other end is the bottom. That's your baby."

I was really excited now. I showed everyone the picture. "See, spine, head, bottom…baby!" I don't know how many times my wife would take a look at the picture and then tell me, "That's upside-down." She understood the picture completely. Then she would try to teach me. "You see," she'd say, "THIS is the head and THIS the bottom. Do you see that now?" I'd look but finally I just told her, "I really can't tell the difference." She said, "Well, I hope that doesn't mean he'll take after *you*."

    After the ultrasound the doctor sat down with my wife and told her what to expect over the next nine months. He discussed the risks involved based on her age, medical and family history. Then he told her what he wanted her to do to minimize those risks. There were vitamins to take, exercises to perform and a strict schedule of office visits. Still, he never said that if she did all those things that the risk factor would drop to zero. Risk is a part of pregnancy no matter what you do. If I said I didn't think about those risks, I'd be lying. I thought about them. I prayed about them. I was concerned about my wife's health and the health of our child, yet, that wasn't how we behaved. Most remarkably, it wasn't how Suzanna behaved.

I watched her over the next few months and although there were some rough days, for the most part she seemed to be having a very positive experience. She was smiling, picking out baby furniture, trying out names and having parties. I was the one showing the anxiety. I kept thinking about the risks, the responsibilities, how little I knew about babies, the state of our finances and the state of the world.

Every few weeks there would be another celebration with gifts. You might think that helped me feel better, but the gifts themselves became a source of anxiety. There was a lot of gear but I didn't know what any of this stuff was for. I remember opening one big box that said "Diaper Genie". I had no idea. I knew it had something to do with diapers, but beyond that I was clueless. Did it make diapers, change them, dress your kid up like Barbara Eden or what? I figured my wife would know, though.

So, I thanked the nice people who gave it to us and as soon as they walked away Suzanna leaned over and whispered, "What's *that*?" I said, "Honey, I don't know either, but let's not rub it, ok?" Hey, I figured if there really is such a thing as a diaper-genie, I don't want anything he's giving away.

"Do I get three wishes?"

"No, just one and two. That's all I do."

I learned later that the Diaper Genie (by Playtex) was really a pretty handy device. It's a large canister that has a double lid and inside is a long continuous white plastic bag. When you have a used diaper you just flip the top up, shove the diaper in and give it a twist and the diaper is sealed in plastic. It worked great for the first two days or so. Then I tried to put in another diaper and it just wouldn't go.

I said, "I think the Diaper Genie is broken," and my wife said, "No, it just needs to be emptied."

"Emptied?" I said. "Not unless it came with gloves and a neoprene suit."

But through all the months of the pregnancy, Suzanna was radiant. It was just like the old clichés we've all heard about expectant mothers having a certain glow. It was true. I couldn't sleep at night for all the glowing. And I had to wonder why. Why—knowing all the risks and uncertainties—was she so able to be so happy and enthusiastic?

I puzzled about it like the Grinch wondering why Christmas came to Whoville even without packages, boxes or bags. Finally I understood. Suzanna had made a choice. For better or worse, the results we get are determined by the choices we make.

Now, her choice probably wasn't a conscious choice. She didn't need to appoint a committee to reach a consensus. It was just a simple choice of *focus*. What did she choose to focus upon? She could have focused on the risks or the responsibilities or even the uncertain future of the world. Instead, she chose to focus on the hope of life that would come at the end of all that waiting.

I believe that that focus positively influenced the outcome, but I'm not asking you to believe that. Just admit this, that such a choice of positive focus improves the emotional experience of *now*. Because of our positive focus, we had nine months of joy, celebration, and anticipation instead of nine months of fear, anxiety, and dread. The emotional experience we derived from each moment was a direct result of what we focused upon. We didn't necessarily lower the risks nor did we deny them. We just allowed ourselves to celebrate the best possible outcome and so we had many days of joy before we ever even met our new baby.

After nine months, the day finally came and my wife went into labor. She was in labor for a long time—33 hours. Now, if you're a mother, you probably made a little exclamation or maybe a low whistle there. My wife thanks you. If you're a man, I doubt that you even paused. You know why? Because if you thought about it at all it was likely a thought like, "Hmmph. Thirty-three hours? What's the big deal? I did 37 straight hours in the La-Z-Boy just last weekend. Say, that's basically the same position, too."

I don't pretend to understand what a mother goes through in childbirth, but I can tell you this. It is time measured on a whole different level. I tried my best to understand at the time. I even asked other new mothers to describe the experience.

I remember asking a friend of mine, a young woman I taught high school with named Joyce who had just had a baby, to explain what labor was like. Joyce was a no-nonsense kind of person who didn't mind being blunt, and something about my question apparently irritated her. She looked me up and down like I was some new species of insect and then raised one eyebrow and said, "You want *me* to explain labor to *you?*" Then she did some kind of cobra thing with her head that scared me to death.

"Yes," I said, "but you can't touch me."

I explained that I was just trying to understand and to be as supportive as I could be of my wife. Joyce responded, "You are not *equipped* to understand what labor is like." Not equipped, I thought? Where do I get this equipment? She continued, "You don't understand *pain*."

Now there I had to disagree. I understand pain plenty. I've had root canals. I've broken bones. I once politely smiled and nodded while I listened for an hour to a friend's Morrisey album and I'm a Cleveland Browns fan. I know pain.

All these were pale imitations of the pain of labor, according to Joyce. She asked me to come up with the single worst pain I'd ever experienced in my life. I really had to think because I've hurt myself in so many creative ways. I've hurt myself with power tools, household appliances and I once had an incident with a Bunsen burner in science class that filled the room with the smell of singed hair and left me looking surprised for three weeks.

But the worst physical pain was way back when I was 12 years old. I had a bike back then that I loved. If you're not old enough to remember the bikes in the 1970s, they were called Stingray bikes. Mine was fire orange with glittery paint, a banana seat, high-rise handlebars and a sissy bar and I could make that bike fly. On the first warm day of spring I was out on my bike really pushing the envelope. I must have been going about 250 miles per hour but from all the freeze and thaw of the departing winter a chunk of pavement had come loose leaving a deep pothole. That hole was deep enough to swallow about half of my front tire. It was a jolt hard enough that I slipped right off my banana seat. Now, you know that bar they have on boys' bikes, the one that runs from under the seat to the handlebars (whose idea was *that*)? When I hit that bar full-straddle, I told Joyce that was the worst pain I ever had.

She said, "Ok, do that every *twelve minutes*!"

Now you men reading this are saying, "Ooohh, so *that's* what labor is like." Men get very sympathetic when you talk about an injury in that vicinity. Battle hardened trauma surgeons who can reattach severed limbs with dispassionate efficiency will cringe in empathetic agony the first time they wheel in a farmer who was kicked in the groin by his cow.

So my wife was in labor for 33 hours. Four-and-a-half hours were spent in "hard" labor. It's probably a good thing no one told my wife that the first 28 and a half hours were the "easy" part. Hard labor is the part where the pushing happens. I never saw anything like that. I was of no use whatever. After awhile I was feeding *myself* the ice chips and moaning, "Make it stop!"

I think I failed as "coach". That's what they told me I was, "the coach." If there are any fathers-to-be reading this, let me just disabuse you of the notion that you're coaching anything in the delivery room. It's just something they tell us so we think we have a job to do and stay out of their way.

I began to suspect that my coaching wasn't of critical importance when I realized that my primary purpose in that room was to remind my wife to *breathe*. I didn't leave the room for 33 hours for fear that she would suffocate without me in the room saying, "Breathe NOW! And NOW!"

I attended the Lamaze classes with my wife. I think it's actually *L'amaze* which is French for "It's amazing" as in, "It's amazing that anyone would willingly choose to go through childbirth without drugs." The instructor gave us coaches a list of supplies to bring to the hospital. One of the strangest items was "a small stuffed animal." What was that for? It was, the instructor explained, a "focal point" for my wife as she suffered through the pain of labor. To me it sounded more like a good way to get myself killed.

There I was in the birthing suite with my wife who was by then in her 30th hour of labor and I'm holding up a little fuzzy duck and saying, "Here's your *focal point*, honey." I could tell she was thinking, "Oh, I *have* a focal point!" Instinctively, the duck and I took a step back.

At the end of 33 hours, it happened. In a moment everything changed. An immeasurable beat of time separated our lives into two parts. On one side was our lives up to that point and on the other was parenthood and all the terrifying wonder and breathless joy that comes with it.

In that moment all those sounds of pain and effort from my wife suddenly changed to sounds of amazement, and love, and certainly relief. My son, Alex weighed into the world at 8 lbs. 13.8 ounces. While I realize that's not the biggest baby ever born, that's still the equivalent of passing a good-sized ham. For the first five minutes of his life I just stood there looking at down at him and thinking "That can't be. Happy Easter, honey!" It's truly a miracle.

The experience also made me appreciate a little more how much a woman has to be subjected to bring a child into the world. In the hours leading up to delivery there is no modesty or privacy. People are coming in and out of the room all the time doing examinations and offering opinions.

"So, has she dilated?"

"No, why, are you an OB?"

"I'm the head custodian."

"GET OUT OF HERE!"

When, I held my new son, Alex David Caperton, for the first time, I saw the path of my life clearly. Beginning in that moment of pure joy I realized that I held in my arms a new focus that would change everything. In that moment when expectancy became life, when potential became reality, when the abstract became the actual and affection was finally introduced to its object, our lives and the universe in which we lived them changed forever. We had become parents. We had a new focus and that focus would change everything. Every priority we had would be reexamined. Every decision would need to evaluated for its impact on this new life. A new focus changed us, our perceptions and our world. It also allowed us to appreciate the value and meaning in every experience. It was a fresh perspective on life and it made everything new.

Chapter 8
Heigh-Ho, Heigh-Ho
(It's Up to You, You Know)

From the time our son, Alex, was a baby, it was clear that he had a love for music. When music played, he got excited. It didn't matter if it was Raffi or Rachmaninoff. If there was a melody and a rhythm, he danced and smiled and laughed.

His favorite, though, was the *Heigh-Ho* song from **Snow White and the Seven Dwarfs**. As soon as that first "heigh-HOOOO" sounded, he would kick his feet and wave his arms and laugh. Consequently, we played that one for him often, and if we weren't close to the DVD player, we sang it. But when we sang it, instead of getting excited, he would relax. So we sang him off to sleep with Heigh-Ho every night, and for every nap throughout the day. Whenever he was distressed, "Heigh-Ho" was the first response. If he woke up from a bad dream, "Heigh-Ho". If he was tired and cranky, "Heigh-Ho".

It was the remedy for all his stresses. Now if you're thinking, "What do you mean, stress? He was a baby. All of his needs were taken care of for him. Babies don't have stress!" Not so. Babies live in a constant state of stress because babies are in a constant state of change. Think about it for a moment. What is the baby experience? You have no perceived control over your life. There's a language barrier. The world is populated by giants. Huge faces come looming up at you constantly, babbling nonsense. You're being fed liquefied foods that starving dogs wouldn't touch. You are bounced, rocked, swung and endlessly patted. Then, every 20 minutes or so, someone comes over and rips your pants off! And the baby just lies there like a miniature Jerry Seinfeld thinking, "What was THAT about?" It's stressful being a baby.

Consequently, "Heigh-Ho" became one of his first words and often we'd hear him call it out in the middle of the night. Then either Suzanna or I would leap from our bed, run into his room, scoop him up in our arms and start softly singing, "Heigh-ho, heigh-ho. It's off to sleep we go…" And within anywhere between 10 minutes and 2 hours, he would.

If you do this enough consecutive nights between 1 and 6am, as I did, you will find yourself in crowded elevators in city buildings crooning, "Heigh-ho, heigh-ho…" And so it became a verb. 'Heigh-ho: *v.i.* - to rock or walk about with a crying infant singing a dwarf song in an effort to induce slumber.'

I had breakfast with a friend of mine one day during this time and after we sat down in our booth at the restaurant he took a look at the extra baggage under my eyes and asked me,

"Were you 'heigh-ho-ing' last night?"

"Until 5 this morning, yeah," I said.

I thought later, "I wonder what the other people in the restaurant thought we were talking about?"

Then my friend said, "I'll bet you'll be glad when that's over, huh?"

That woke me up. I hadn't really given any thought to it ever being over. It was just a routine and routines tend to create the illusion of permanence. So I thought about his question and then I answered, "No. Maybe if we had four kids it wouldn't be the same answer, but we don't. You know why? Because he needs me right now in a way that he'll never need me again. He'll need me in other ways, I know, but this is special."

Since that day, that particular need he had for me is long past. He's in his 20s and towers four inches over his dad. If I tried to attempt a heigh-ho walk with him now I'd need a truss before I made the second step. Still, I think of the patterns I wore in the carpet night after night as I sang a silly song over and over again into the darkness with the soft warmth of my infant son curled against my shoulder and I realize that I miss those days very much. I know now what a privilege I was given then. How sad it would be if my memories of those nights that seemed so long yet sped by so quickly were tinged with the regret that I had complained about that privilege while it was still mine to enjoy.

Of course sometimes we all forget to see the privilege in our responsibilities as we focus on the work before us. I have wailed in pain and anger as I've pried a little green Army man from the sole of my bare foot after trying to navigate my son's room in the dark, wondering (very) aloud why there are always toys all over the floor. On those occasions my wife would remind me that a someday when there wouldn't be was already on the road. For a moment then I would forget the red welt on my foot and visualize a room neat and devoid of the happy aftermath of a child's play, and the drifts of action figures and cars would no longer look so bad.

Those two stories underscore what is perhaps the most powerful ability that human beings possess to unlocking happiness and joy in the now. That unique ability is our capacity to decide the meaning of what happens in our lives. We often confuse ourselves by talking about our experiences as if they arrive with a fixed value of good or bad, but that's not so. Everything that happens to us places us somewhere on a continuum between joy and pain. Except for the rare tragedy or off-the-charts triumph, most experiences will fall in the mundane gray area in between. With few exceptions, you get to decide whether what happens is pain or joy. It's a matter of what you focus upon; the short term pain of lost sleep or extra work or perhaps the long term joy of the good you get to do for someone else and the memories you create for yourself.

Most of the time we don't think about why we feel as we do about our experiences and are probably unaware that we're even making an evaluation. So we become convinced that experiences arrive with a fixed value. But if we slow down that process a little, we see where we sometimes cheat ourselves out of all the joy and happiness available to us every day. The process goes something like this:

>!. Something happens
>2. It passes through mental/emotional filters
>3. You assess whether the event moves you toward or away from your goals.
>4. You choose a response based on your conclusions
>5. Your chosen response determines an outcome

How we decide what our experiences mean is almost certainly an infinitely more complicated process than the six steps above, but these steps give you a sense of how subjective life can be and therefore how much more control you have than you might think.

When a couple discovers that they're having a baby, they go through a process of assessment before it really becomes the "joyous event" that it's purported to be on the New Baby cards at Hallmark. Let's take a look at how it progresses from neutral biological phenomenon to joyous event in five easy steps:

1. Something happens – If I have to explain this part you need to get down to Borders and buy "Reproduction for Dummies"
2. Filters begin to shape the experience. Were they trying to have a baby? If so, it's slam-dunk, mission accomplished, we're number one! If not, things get more complicated. You begin to strain the information through filters to determine how you feel. Personal filters might include: Do I like kids? Do I think I'll make a good parent? Do I see a hopeful future? Are we financially stable? Do I anticipate a positive response from my family, my friends, and my employer?
3. Does the filtered perception of the event move you in the direction of your goals? Hopefully you can see yourself as a proud parent attending school plays and dance recitals and soccer games with iPhone camera clicking away. You can see the hugs and hear a child's laughter and their comical bewilderment as you steal noses and produce quarters from ears. You project yourself into a Christmas-yet-to-come where you'll eat the cookies *and* the carrots left for Santa and his reindeer as you clumsily put together bikes and doll houses, screaming into your sleeve every time your scrape another layer of skin off your knuckles. You might also see the fevers and the braces and college savings intercepting the money you were going to use to put in a pool someday, but if the images agree with an imagined future where you'll be happy and fulfilled and surrounded by grandchildren in the shadowy mists of someday, you'll conclude that the experience of parenthood is generally a very good thing indeed and that it really is consistent with your goals and

therefore you can move to the next step in this process which is:

4. Choose a response that is positive and in agreement with the greeting card assessment that the arrival of a new baby is, for you at least, a joyous event which will finally

5. Create the outcome of celebration in the short term and dedication to your parental responsibilities in the longer term.

Let's say someone has different filters installed. They can see only expense and sleepless nights and the struggle of finding a baby sitter every time they want to eat in a restaurant without a drive thru. Are they wrong? Well, no, but certainly future experiences starting with the baby's first finger-grab may challenge their conclusions and the subjective value of their experience may change.

Chapter 9
Humor as a Tool

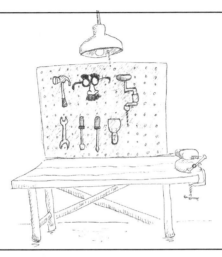

As a parent, I learned more about the things I speak about to organizations than I could have learned in any classroom anywhere in the world. I learned lessons in happiness, love, patience, communication and how humor can help.

I've done seminars on the importance of humor to enhance communication and to improve engagement. You won't find a better example of the importance of humor in how we relate to others than in your experience as a parent of a small child.

If you're a parent, think back to those early days and remember how you used to interact with your children when they were just infants. You used humor, didn't you? You made funny faces, you put things on your head, and you made flatulent noises on their bellies and resorted to foolishness that made Carrot Top look like Noel Coward by comparison.

What did they do? Mostly nothing. They stared at you with all the good humor of Vladimir Putin. Did that slow you down? No. You crossed your eyes and talked like a duck and spun the poor little tyke around until he spit up and you just kept performing like Jerry Lewis on Ritalin withdrawal.

Finally, after months of your pathetic slapstick, the payoff came: the smile. When that baby responded to your lame humor with a smile it made all your undignified antics worthwhile., didn't it? Think about that for just a moment. The first clear emotional message that a child sends is related to humor.

"Wait a minute," you might be thinking, "the *first* emotional message? Isn't their first emotional message *crying*?"

It only seems that way because of the meaning we later attach to crying. But, crying can mean a lot of things. Mostly, though, it means, "I have a need." As new parents we struggle to fulfill that need at first. The baby cries and we rush to do something but we don't know what. "What do you need? Rocked, fed, burped, diapered, held? Give me a clue. One word, a syllable, sounds-like, anything at all."

Eventually we work it out. Sometimes we get pretty advanced in understanding the nuances in their cries. "You hear that? That's a hungry cry," or "that's a wet diaper cry." Parents are like Windtalkers, "Two short sobs and a wail. That's a doody diaper and her bottle's gotten cold."

When that baby smiles at us, though, there's no translation needed. We go all gooshy inside and then post on Facebook. The first time Alex smiled at me I called people up and told them. "He smiled at me. He loves me." I knew it was true. It was all there in his smile and I told other people so.

Of course there is always someone who wants to spoil it for you. One person you tell about that first smile and what does she tell you? "It's just gas" (we're back to that again).

The first person who told me that, I'll admit I got a little angry. "It is NOT just gas," I said. "If that were true, Taco Bell would be the happiest place on earth, wouldn't it? People would be smiling all over that restaurant.

"Looks like life is good for you, sir."

"No, I just had the burrito grande."

We would avoid happy people if that were the case, wouldn't we? "He's smiling! RUN!"

Research into the emotional development of infants suggests that they really do experience joy and humor at a much earlier age than the experts once believed possible. You didn't have to tell me that, though. I know the difference between a smile and a burp.

That smile is not just a humor response; it is the *primary* humor response. Whenever you're in an interaction with another person and humor is present, isn't your first reaction to that humor a smile? I know it's not always the case, of course. There are some people who just laugh with no smile or warning of any kind. They just go from completely serious to "HA HA HA HA HA!" with no warning. It can be kind of creepy.

Most of us follow a more standard progression. We smile and then the smile gets broader. Eventually laughter bubbles up. Did you know that we don't even really fully understand what laughter is? One research article I read described laughter as a *respiration pattern*. What? Respiration pattern? No, laughter is nothing less than a force of nature as irresistible as gravity or the tides. Have you ever found yourself in a situation where it was really inappropriate to laugh and yet you *had* to laugh? So you tried to hold it in and discovered it will find another exit. And it will take stuff with it, too.

If the humor response continues to be stimulated, the laughter gets stronger, even violent. You experience temporary muscular paralysis, tears stream down your face and finally you lose bladder control. That's it, stage one through stage four. I always say if I can bring an audience to incontinence, I've won. I've done my job well. I want people to say, "When he finished there wasn't a dry seat in the house."

It all begins with a smile, the primary humor response. Consider this, a smile is universal, it transcends language, and—as you've perhaps experienced with your own children—it precedes language as well. A smile communicates joy, openness and caring not only to those you know, but also to strangers outside your own community or culture.

Pretty basic stuff, I'll admit, yet we need to be reminded from time to time. Something happens to us at some point growing up when laughter and seeking joy isn't automatic anymore. It's really no wonder. How many times while we were growing up did some well-meaning adult tell you to "get serious" and "wipe that smile off your face"?

It isn't that we are any less able to enjoy laughter than we were as children, but many of us have had our natural tendency for laughter conditioned out of us. To what degree are we less likely to enjoy laughter as grown-ups than we did as kids? Recently published figures comparing adults and children demonstrated a dramatic change in how most adults lose their fluency in the language of laughter. How many times each day do you suppose an adult laughs on average? The answer: 15 times. Now, that may be good news for you. You might be thinking, "Hey, 15 times? That's almost one for every waking hour. Would you look at that, it's almost time for my chuckle." But compare that figure to typical preschoolers. How many times each day do they laugh on average? You know it's more than 15, but what would you guess? Thirty times? Fifty? One hundred times? Would you believe, *400 times a day!* It's true. No wonder they don't hold jobs at that age.

By the way, I'm not suggesting that you laugh 400 times a day. Whatever you do for a living you wouldn't do it for long. They'd put you in a secure room and people with clipboards would come and look at you through a little round in the door. Still, I think it is important that we ask ourselves, "How did 385 daily expressions of joy disappear, and how can I get a few of those back?"

The short answer is, you have to make it a priority again. It has to be of enough importance to us that we'll go seek out joy instead of just waiting around for it to happen to us. We want joy and we like to laugh, but we often are pretty passive about finding it. Unlike kids who go out in search of enjoyment, we treat joy as an unearned bonus. Like a favorite uncle who we'd like a visit from but it never quite occurs to us to go see him.

I think we could learn a lot from watching children and trying to remember what we knew back then. For one thing we weren't afraid to seek out joy and to play. It is funny when you think about it but the way we behave during the most wonderful time of our lives—childhood—is considered certifiable behavior if we engage in it as adults. If a man of 43 cries when he gets hungry or if he dances in front of a three way mirror at the department store or if a middle-aged woman lies down on the floor of the bank when the line is too long and boring they might soon find themselves sharing a room with the guy who laughs 400 times a day.

It's not about ridiculous and impulsive behavior. It's about realizing that when we grew out of immaturity we also may have purged some of the precious gifts of childhood: playfulness, laughter, creativity and a genuine enthusiasm for being alive.

One October years ago I was out with my son for trick or treat. He was dressed as a mad scientist complete with a lab coat, surgical gloves and green spiky hair. I think I had more fun than he did. The streets in our neighborhood swarmed with princesses, monsters, and superheroes. I noticed something else, too. The grown-ups were really enjoying themselves. Almost every adult wore a smile as we shepherded our little ghosts, monsters, and Captain Americas from house to house. We were all reliving our own old trick-or-treat days vicariously through our kids.

I really had the urge to don a clown nose, grab a pillowcase and hit a few of the houses myself. I could remember the excitement I felt as a kid at Halloween. I'd get my costume on complete with the celluloid mask which made it impossible to see and nearly impossible to breathe (remember getting your tongue stuck in the little mouth slot?).

When you think about childhood experiences like Trick-or-Treat you can understand why childhood is such a confusing time. It's such a contradiction of what our parents tell us the rest of the year. What do we preach to our kids all the time? "Don't cross streets, don't talk to people you don't know, always be polite." And then October 31st rolls around and we say, "Ok, slip this mask on and now with your vision obstructed we want you to wander in and out of traffic after dark and demand candy from strangers. That's for tonight only, though. Tomorrow we're right back to considerate and safety-conscious."

When you really think about it, childhood is really the only time in you life you can get away with something like that. You've got a mask, a bag, and you're telling people to fill it with things you like. At six years old, that's Trick or Treat. At 36, that's a felony.

"What are you in for?"

"Trick or treating."

"Oh yeah?"

"Yeah. Apparently, there's some kind of rule against that at Bob's Liquor Store."

For all of it's contradictions, though, Halloween is an opportunity for us to remember a little of that joy of living reserved for kids young enough to put on a Batman costume and plastic mask and, without a trace of self-consciousness, go out trick or treating.

I will add that the holiday isn't quite as exclusively the little kids' experience that I remember. It seems that more and more people on the wrong side of puberty are horning in. This year I saw some of them actually driving from house to house. I had one "kid" 6'3" with a hockey mask and a bloody machete. I thought, "There's no way I'm giving him candy." I wrote him a check.

So humor is such a huge part of childhood that preschoolers laugh about 25 times more than grown-ups. Maybe that means that humor is important to our development or maybe at four we're just really easy to entertain. But while we may not be a very tough audience at four years old, throughout our lives humor appears early and remains critical to our healthy mental, emotional, and social well being. Why else would laughter appear at such a young age—long before speech—in our development?

Humor is not only an emotional facet of human beings, it's also a form of communication that's so fundamental to how we connect with others that it precedes language in the early years of our lives and for the rest of our lives it transcends it. People who are great communicators usually have a highly developed sense of humor. When someone has humor in the communication arsenal he or she is better equipped to defuse conflict, form connections with others and to solve problems than the person who is humor-impaired.

The humor-skilled person can use humor to break tension in tough situations. She connects more easily with others and—by using humor—can open pathways of communication that can help forge innovative solutions. After all, when we talk about creativity we're talking about a process that is best described as mental playfulness. It's taking the what-if questions and removing boundaries for the answers. That description also works for humor, which is an emotionally creative process.

Maybe the reason why we need reminders of the importance of humor and creativity in our adult years is that sense that we know we once had something valuable that we lost along the way. We may not remember laughing 400 times a day, but we know that we once experienced more joy and happiness than we do now. We may not know exactly when we stopped being creative, but we recall that there was a time when we could not only imagine the impossible, we could color it, too.

The loss of creativity and the ultimate reduction of our levels of joy is one of the toughest things about growing up. Sure, some of that is just inevitable as we learn that there are limits to possibility. Learning that Santa Claus, the Easter Bunny or the Tooth Fairy are only figurative realities is a sad but necessary rite of passage and most of us can remember the period of doubting when we tried so hard to resist logic in order to cling to our childhood fantasies.

I remember when I was about 7 or 8 years old and I was just starting to feel a little less than convinced about the Jolly Old Elf (ok, I was 14). I heard Mom and Dad talking about the crush of the Christmas bills and I started wondering why there were bills at all if Santa brought all the Christmas presents. For a while I thought I had it worked out. Santa didn't give the gifts for free, I thought, he just sold them to Mom and Dad for a discount.

I clung to my Santa-the-Wholesaler fantasy desperately enough to get through one more Christmas with my childhood intact but the very next year I saw Santa having a smoke break in the employees lounge at the department store where we shopped and the jig was up. Santa might puff a pipe, but Pall Malls? Never.

Once you've crossed the border that separates the never-land of childhood from the sober world of grown-ups you may think that rekindling our childlike imagination as unlikely as rekindling your belief in Santa. But unlike our trust in Kris Kringle, imagination and joy are still relevant and available to us if we just know where to look.

Chapter 10
Using What God Gave You

I once went to one of those dinner shows that take place in a horse arena and present either a medieval knight's contest or a Buffalo Bill type wild west show while the audience members divide their attention between eating and cheering and trying to keep the arena dust off of their vegetable medleys.

We took my Aunt Thelma with us and as we were served our roasted chicken, the servers instructed us to "use the utensils God gave you". My aunt looked around her plate bewildered and then remarked to the guy whose job it was to throw bread rolls at the crowd that she hadn't gotten any.

The roll-tosser pointed to her hands and said, "Those! Those are the utensils God gave you!" I guess eating like a toddler was supposed to be part of the charm and the authenticity of the place, or maybe they just had all the investment money tied up in horses and bolo ties and so they couldn't afford real knives and forks.

Using humor is a little like that. When we talk about the benefits of using healing and compassionate humor, some people feel left out because they know that they weren't issued a rapier wit or the ability to tell a joke. To those people I say—to paraphrase the pumpernickel pitcher at the Buffalo Bill Dinner Theater—use the tools God gave you.

If you have a means of communicating, you have the ability to use humor. Remember that a sense of humor isn't the ability to *make* people laugh; it's instead an attitude of lightness that *invites* laughter. When we can invite others to laugh, even (and maybe especially) when it's at our own expense, we're using our sense of humor in a way that is generous and compassionate and even healing for ourselves and for others.

It begins with the primary humor response. Remember that the primary humor response is a smile. That smile is one of the tools that God gave you to communicate with humor. But it can't be just any smile. It has to be one that communicates joy and elicits a similar humor response from others.

This smile is known as the "Duchenne Smile". You've probably never heard of the Duchenne smile although you might use it every day. The Duchenne smile is the type of smile we associate with real joy and merriment. It's the type of smile that arises naturally in a joyful or humorous situation.

It gets its name from the same 19th century French neurologist, Guillaume Benjamin Amand Duchenne, who identified a certain type of muscular dystrophy that also bears his name. Duchenne studied facial expressions and determined that the reason we can tell the difference between a genuine smile and a forced smile of politeness lies in the subtleties of the facial muscles employed in each case. All smiles typically involve the *zygomaticus major* muscles around the mouth. The Duchenne smile also involves the contraction of the *orbicularis oculi* muscles around the eyes. When the eyes are involved, we recognize the smile as genuine and we respond emotionally to the expression.

Have you ever walked into a doctor's or dentist's office and the receptionist looks up and gives you that professional smirk along with, "fill out the forms and have a seat, please." Do you really feel moved emotionally by that expression or do you just consider it a polite ritual and respond by curling your own lips into an insincere crescent and cooing, "Thank you, I will"?

You don't feel moved because you don't believe that the expression was tied to a sincere emotion, but then along comes someone you know and like and she gives you a smile that reaches from her mouth to her eyes, forming a little network of crinkles around the corners there. Suddenly you feel like smiling back in just the same way. You might even feel a little like laughing. What was the difference? One was just a dutiful smile and left you cold. The other was the Duchenne smile and it moved you to experience joy, perhaps even laughter.

Why should the movement of a few facial muscles have such an emotional impact and why does that matter for you and your own joy? It matters for several reasons. First, the surest way to experience more personal joy is to inspire it in others. Just as the most effective learning method is to teach someone else, so it is with happiness. When I make others feel good, I feel better myself. Joy defies mathematical logic; it is only multiplied when we divide it.

It doesn't even matter if you aren't particularly gifted with language. The most important tool you have for communicating positive emotions to others isn't your words or your great wit.

In face-to-face communication, I have many tools available to me. I have a vocabulary of tens of thousands of words. I have a voice capable of a wide range of pitch, rate, tone, volume and inflection. And I have a body.

In a one-on-one situation, what would you guess is the most important tool you have for conveying attitudes and feelings to the other person? In other words, if you were to take all of your communications tools and assign each one a percentage of the message to carry, which component would do the most work? According to the research of Albert Mehrabian, professor emeritus of psychology at UCLA, the reality is surprising. Although the words we speak are needed to form precise meaning, in a face-to-face communication about feelings and attitudes (as opposed to, say, an exchange about instructions and procedures), the words account for only 7% of the total meaning.

Voice does more of the heavy lifting. Your pitch, volume and rate communicate the meaning of your words significantly. Most men can attest to this fact. How many men in long-term relationships can remember getting into a conflict with your wife or girlfriend, not for *what* you said, but *how you said it*?

It's something that I'll confess I have little control over. My wife can read my voice like a vocal polygraph. There are times when it would be better if I just didn't speak at all because no matter how hard I try to keep my feelings out of my answers, she can see right through an innocent inflection or a diphthong and into the core of my psyche. At times like these it would be better for everyone if I just had a stack of response cards with messages written on them like, "You're right!" "I agree with you!" "I love you!" Instead, I'll try to answer a question without giving away my feelings and suddenly she knows all.

"Now tell me the truth, did you really like your birthday dinner, because it won't hurt my feelings if you didn't? I know you love salmon and I know how much you like curry so when I found that recipe, I thought of you."

"Oh yeah, Good thinking. I didn't even know they had salmon in India. That was really (don't lie, she can detect a lie) *unforgettable*."

Here there is a long silence while the tape of my vocal response is analyzed.

"You didn't like it, did you?"

"Whaaat? I didn't *say* that (you are so busted)"

"I know, but it's not *what* you said, it's *how you said it*." [1]

Add up the percentages of words (7%) and voice (38%) and we have 45% percent of the attitudes/emotions message, leaving 55% to the physical. The physical includes eye contact, facial expressions, *kinesics* (gestures and movement), and *proxemics* (how close you stand during the exchange).

Even the less than hilarious personality can use humor to influence others if he or she uses the primary humor response as part of the all-important 55%. That's why using a smile that has a real perceived emotional value is a useful tool.

---

[1] **This exchange is completely hypothetical as I am not dumb enough to recount an actual domestic disagreement. To my knowledge, my wife has never prepared a curry salmon dish and if she did I'm sure I would love it. You hear that, honey? I would love it!*

I understand that the person reading this could conceivably be a manager or an IT person and thus out of practice with the Duchenne smile, so let's take it step by step.

Find a mirror. Smile at yourself and look at the area around the mouth and eyes. If your smile doesn't really reach the eyes, you're not doing the Duchenne. Raise your eyebrows slightly. Create the wrinkles around the eyes (people who Botox are excused). Maybe open your mouth. Practice your Duchenne smile in the mirror. When you think you have it right, pay attention not only to how you look, but how you feel. Not only does the Duchenne smile elicit a positive emotional response from others, it can improve your own emotional state as well.

Anyone who has studied the process of communication can tell you that there are two basic types of communication: interpersonal and intrapersonal. *Interpersonal* is what is sent and received between myself and other people. *Intrapersonal* communication is what I communicate within myself. Any time I'm sending a message out, I'm also sending it *in* to my subconscious mind that operates in many ways as an entirely separate entity from my conscious mind. This is the basis of Neuro-Linguistic Programming (NLP). The subconscious has no appreciation for the source of a communication. A message of joy, love, or threat can be generated by others or by our own brains, yet the subconscious treats them all the same. When we say hurtful things to ourselves, the subconscious responds with the same distress as if it had come from another person. When we communicate physically—with our facial expression for example—the subconscious triggers a neurochemical response in our brains consistent with the signals it receives from our face, our posture, and our gestures. This connection between the physical and emotional is what is called a *cybernetic loop* relationship.

When I experience an emotion, there will be a physical manifestation of that emotion. That's hardly surprising. When we're happy we smile, when we're sad our shoulders slump and we're literally downcast in our expression. But here's the exciting news. When we want to experience more joy, happiness and enthusiasm, we don't have to wait for an external event. Because of the cybernetic loop relationship that exists between your mind and body, you can assume a different physical attitude and the emotions consistent with that physical sign will tend to follow.

The Duchenne smile doesn't just affect the emotions of others, it affects your own as well. If you want to feel more confident, assume the posture of confidence. If you want less anxiety, banish that expression of terror on your face and smooth the knit brows. And if you want to feel more joy and happiness, try on your Duchenne smile and give it away.

Now I realize that some people are suspicious of the physical/emotional angle as being false or disingenuous. Sometimes I run into that resistance during the exercise itself. Once I was in Illinois doing a program for customer service reps for an Illinois power company. During the Duchenne smile exercise one of the participants, a woman in her 30's, said to her friend, "He's trying to turn us into *phonies*."

I said to her, "You know I can *hear* you."

She apparently didn't care. She answered, "You're trying to make me *pretend* emotions that I don't *feel*. Well, I'm sorry, I'm just not made that way!" And then she closed her eyes and shook her head with a rapid "that's final" sanctimony that reminded me of Dana Carvey's Church Lady.

Was she really so concerned with being authentic and sincere, or was she afraid that she might bear some responsibility for her emotions? I can't say, but if the latter were true, she could no longer totally blame her customers, her colleagues and her company for how she felt and that may have been a higher price than she was willing to pay. For her it might have been easier to live with being miserable because of conditions outside of her control than to believe she was miserable because of her own unwillingness to choose a new response. What this woman was exhibiting was a typical pessimistic view.

Martin Seligman, a professor of Psychology at the University of Pennsylvania and author of **Learned Optimism** (Vintage Books, 2006), says that pessimists differ from optimists in the way that they explain their adversity to themselves. We all encounter adversity, but the pessimist *explains* it by what Seligman calls the "3 Ps".

The first P is for **Personal**. Have you ever ridden with a pessimist along a heavily traveled route and the pessimist starts in complaining (because that's what they do) about the traffic lights?

"Look at that, another red light! That's the third red light. I've been traveling this same road for 18 years and I always get red lights. It doesn't matter what time of day or how fast or slow I go, it's just red lights all the way for me. I hate this road and I hate these lights, blah, blah, blah."

What you should say is, "Are you telling me that you think these lights *know* who you are?"

The pessimist will probably deny believing that, but it's exactly what he thinks, because for him, every adversity is personal.

The second explanation he has for his adversity: it's **Pervasive**. The adversity is never limited to the adversity itself. It's instead just a symptom for the larger curse that is life. Have you ever been around a pessimist when he's entering data on a computer and the computer suddenly freezes up with the data unsaved? Does the pessimist say, "Gee, that's certainly going to be a little inconvenient." No, more likely the pessimist will jump up from the desk and shout, "My life stinks!" It's not just the adversity; it's his *life* that is the problem.

Finally, the pessimist explains the adversity as **Permanent**. This may be the most dangerous explanation of all. It's the rat-in-the-first-cage mentality.

The consequences from these kinds of explanations of adversity are: *hopelessness, helplessness* and *burnout*.

Optimists, by the way, are no happier about adversity than pessimists, but they explain it to themselves in a very different way. I consider myself an optimist, but I'll admit that I've never had a flat tire and then jumped out of the car cheering, "Oh boy! Now I get to use my Triple-A membership!" I'm not happy about the adversity but I explain it to myself differently than a pessimist would. Rather than *personal, pervasive and permanent*, optimists explain their challenges and setbacks as *random, limited and temporary*. That little adjustment in the way we explain our difficulties to ourselves may be a minor distinction, but it's a distinction that makes a big difference.

Chapter 11
Elimination is the Key

Mr. Wilcox was one of the most memorable people I've ever met. He was a gemologist who owned and operated a store called The Rock Shop on the bustling and garish main strip of Gatlinburg, Tennessee. Gatlinburg lies at the entrance to the Great Smoky Mountains National Park where idyllic streams cascade over ancient rocks and hiking trails provide an escape route from the chaos of modern civilization. But in Gatlinburg, that chaos literally presses right up against the boundary line between the natural beauty of the park and the gaudy environs of a true tourist trap town. The result is a surreal juxtaposition of people and nature. Gatlinburg is basically a traffic jam surrounded by restaurants, tee shirt stores and wax museums.

Sandwiched between all the flashing neon motel signs and identical trinket and souvenir shops was a small store that sold jewelry fashioned from every kind of mineral and stone you might find on planet Earth. When I was a kid we would visit the Smoky Mountains and I could always count on a few hours in The Rock Shop looking at shelves of fossils and amethyst geodes while my mother and grandmother examined the rings and necklaces and bracelets that were displayed in a rectangle of connected glass cases at the center of the store. Within that glass rectangle was a man who for decades was as much a fixture of the store as the display cases of quartz crystals.

Mr. Wilcox seemed very old when I was a child of five, and when I visited in my thirties with my wife, he was still there and just as active and enthusiastic as ever. I reminded him of my mother and my grandmother who had come so often to the store and he remembered them clearly and described my two sisters as well. I knew it was rude, but I had to ask him how old he was. He proudly declared that he was almost 90, and admitted that he still worked 40 or more hours a week on his feet the whole time. I guess when you stand next to 100 million year-old fossils all day, 90 seems downright juvenile.

I expressed some interest in a few items in the case and he produced each gem with a story of where it came from, what forces had shaped it, and what unique properties each stone possessed. He was passionate about his work, obviously successful and apparently very happy. I saw an opportunity to learn from someone who had the wisdom of a lifetime and the successful result of whatever philosophy had guided him on his journey, so I asked him, "Mr. Wilcox, you're so healthy and lively and you seem to be a happy person, could I ask what you consider your secret?"

Mr. Wilcox, nodded his head, "Absolutely, I'll tell you exactly what it is." Then he heightened the drama by beckoning me closer as if it really were a secret he didn't want everyone to know about. I leaned in and turned one ear to him and he said in a low voice, "*Elimination* is the key."

I blinked. "Elimination? You mean . . ." I started.

"Irregularity will kill you!" he said solemnly.

Okay, it wasn't exactly the Eureka moment I was anticipating. I expected something lofty and philosophical and instead I got a pitch to eat more fiber. I had to chuckle a little at that, but in the years since Mr. Wilcox shared that pearl of wisdom, I've reflected on it, and not just for the reasons you think. If you consider it, the survival of every living organism relies on its ability to get fuel and to eliminate waste. I read an interesting factoid just the other day that more *drosophilae* (fruit flies) die from constipation than from any other cause, which is weird because you'd think with all that *fruit*. I mean *cheese* flies I could understand, but fruit flies?

If you've ever had a bout of fruit fly's complaint, you know how miserable the body feels when that part of the system is down. You feel out of balance, slow, and bloated. Did you ever consider that you sometimes need an emotional, mental, and spiritual colonic as well? We hold on to painful memories when they're no longer of any use but to cause us misery. We ruminate over our failures, we fret about what isn't happening or often what isn't even likely to happen. We watch disturbing images on TV, we think thoughts of failure, we get so busy with minutiae that don't make time to tend to our spiritual needs or even to tell the people we care about how much we love them. We feel empty and void and yet our brains are stuffed with entertainment, anxieties, regrets, and self-doubt. We're constipated in ways that are far more hazardous than any physical back-up.

When we get to the point when the physical digestive system can't retain any more, the body can take some unpleasantly strong action to set itself to rights. The mind and spirit though, are another matter. There's almost no limit to what crud and junk can be stored in there so you have to resolve to be more selective about what you take in. You'll find that as you start putting the right things in your mind and spirit, the sludge gets flushed out (I apologize for any unfortunate image that description may have conjured).

I heard a speaker once observe that when you squeeze lemons and oranges they will only produce what's inside. Whatever we have inside, he pointed out, will be expressed when we're under pressure. We may think we're balanced, loving, positive and spiritually complete, but when the pressure starts to squeeze us from all sides, whatever we've fills our minds and hearts with will start to flow. If it's envy, we'll get resentment. If it's hatred, we'll get anger. But if we've really fed our spirit and mind with joy and kindness and faith, then in our time of distress and pressure we'll have our hope and love to sustain us.

Tim Ferris is a young entrepreneur and the author of the best-selling book, **The Four-Hour Work Week**. In it, Ferris lays out a four-step plan to creating an automated income stream to enable a lifestyle built around realizing the individual's dreams as an alternative to waiting for retirement to escape the daily grind. One of the four steps in his process is elimination of the things that take 80% of our time and produce 20% of our rewards. He recommends going on a "low-information diet" during which you don't surf the web, watch news or read the paper. It's a good exercise and a real eye-opener when we realize how much time is consumed getting information for which we have no real use except to entertain or to cause us unnecessary anxiety.

I like keeping up with the news of the world, but I have taken an important step in my information intake routine: I don't watch the late-night local news. I made this decision for a couple of reasons. First, there is always morning news when I get up so I haven't really missed anything I need to know. Secondly, almost all the news is bad anyway. Think about it for a moment. What is the 11 o'clock news? It's every bad, terrible, horrible, awful thing that happened anywhere in the world compressed into one half hour just before you go to sleep. It's good to know *what* is going on, but it's also important to decide *when* you should know it.

Media is so ubiquitous that it's hard to escape. There are some things that I recommend avoiding altogether. Programs that just take a glass-bottomed boat tour through the sewers of human behavior are—in my humble opinion—as bad for your soul as cigarettes are for your lungs and heart. Then there are pundits who work in outrage and anger like Picasso worked in oils and pastels. There's no spark of cultural or political controversy so small that they can't fan it into a conflagration of national indignation and raging demagoguery. When we think of the polarization of America, we have these guys to thank for much of it.

Other entertainment and information sources are a judgment call for each individual. Some people love doctor shows or police dramas, but I start to imagine I have all the symptoms from the doctor programs and I'm convinced that half the crimes reported on the nightly news were cribbed from cop show scripts.

With movies people tend to be more discerning in their viewing because it requires money and a specific intention to go see one. Still, it seems there are more poor choices than good ones. When my wife and I go to the movies we enjoy watching the coming attractions. Watching the trailers is my third favorite part of going to the movies, after popcorn and Twizzlers. Making a trailer is a separate cinematic art form and I appreciate a good one. Too many of them are better than the movies themselves with great editing and graphics.

After each preview, my wife and I go through a quick evaluation process where we turn to each other in the dim theater and exchange a nod, a shrug or a head shake. If we open our eyes widely while rapidly nodding our heads, it means the movie has made our short list of films we'll want to see. If we shrug and turn our palms up it means that it has potential but at best it's going to be a Netflix choice.

Most movie trailers will get the head shake, which of course means, "Not even if you paid me." Features sure to get the shake include any title with a Roman numeral larger than II in the title, anything showing scenes of actors leaping in slow motion away from explosions or cars being inexplicably launched into the air, and any story set in a bleak post-apocalyptic world where all survivors fight for water or fuel but apparently still go to the gym regularly. Add to that any plot that turns on the main character's ability to do things that are physically impossible like stop time, fly, read minds, converse with animals or ghosts that no one else can see, or—in the case of John Travolta—speak with a Bosnian accent.

Finally, and most importantly, any film that deals with a kidnapped child. For that last one we don't even wait for the end of the clip. All we need is the narrator to say, "A child is *missing*. . ." and we are shaking our heads like someone just offered us escargot. We know it's just a movie, but from the moment we became parents, we became unable to endure even a dramatic portrayal of a parent's worst fear. It's just not for us.

With omnipresent video, though we don't have to settle for the dramatic CGI portrayals of mayhem on the big screen or forensic dramas where actors are auditioned to lie still on a stainless steel table. Now we have real blood and gore in reality programs that present actual human suffering as just another entertainment choice. Again, there might be some edifying aspect to some of them, but for me they are must-not-see-TV.

When the reality trend was just getting popular, and I was a little less selective in my viewing choices, I happened upon a program on The Learning Channel that changed everything. The program was called: *Trauma, Life in the ER*. It was one of the most disturbing hours of TV I ever watched and I'll never forget it although I wish I could. The installment I saw was one they later used in their promos so it was kind of their signature episode. In this segment there was, no kidding, a man in the ER who had a 9-inch knife in his *head!* I'm not making this up. Right in the top of his head, buried to the hilt, a knife. They showed an x-ray of his skull with this long knife right in the top. Now, I don't know much about medicine, but do you really need an x-ray to tell you what the trouble is there?

"Well, Bob, we got the x-rays back and we think we've diagnosed your trouble. According to these it seems you have a big knife in your head, you see that there? We're almost positive that *is* your problem."

I don't remember how they explained it got there. I don't think it was accidental although I suppose it could have just been a bad night at a Japanese restaurant. I'm guessing that it was a crime and I'm assuming that they are looking for a tall assailant, but I really can't recall because I was just so horrified at the image of this handle sticking out of this poor man's head like a stick in a candy apple.

The hard part of this whole thing was that they didn't know how to remove it. It wasn't like you could walk up and yank it out like Arthur and Excalibur or something. The knife was lodged in his brain and the slightest touch could result in death or paralysis. So they brought together a team of neurosurgeons and they conferred over their options and one of them actually suggested, "What if we leave it in?" (I'm not sure but that might have been the janitor from maternity) Leave it *in*?

They didn't do that, I'm happy to report. They were able to remove the blade and I believe the patient made pretty impressive recovery, but what if they had gone with that course of action? I don't know how you would even break that news to the patient. What would you do, maybe use a good news/bad news approach?

"Well, Bob, there's good news and bad news. The good news is, your hat's not going to blow off so often . . . but there is a downside. You're going to want to avoid thunderstorms and horseshoe tournaments."

Needless to say, I don't make that program part of my intake anymore.

What are you taking in and what do you think it's doing to you inside? You can deny it all you want, but we tend to become what we behold. If we surround ourselves with images of violence, we're more likely to consider violence in conflict situations. If we indulge our lust with meaningless physical conquests and imagery that objectifies women, we erode our capacity for intimacy and healthy physical relationships. And if we entertain ourselves with constant depictions of the darkest aspects of human depravity and selfishness, we will eventually become cynical and jaded people unable to feel authentic joy and hope.

Of course there are some people like real homicide detectives and trauma nurses who have to see the real dead bodies and the knives in the heads of patients and thank God for them. They are truly heroic for their willingness to confront the horrors that I don't have the courage to face, but ask them and they'll admit how critical their need is to unplug and find balance.

I had the privilege of seeing a presentation by a psychologist and an expert in the psychology of sex offenders and child molesters. He has the unenviable job of consulting on cases sometimes involving the abduction and murder of children. I spoke with him at length after his program and the question that was foremost in my mind was how he maintains his hope and even his sanity in the face of all the evil he must encounter in his job. He discussed a strong faith that helps sustain him and bolsters his sense of purpose even when he deals with heartbreak and horror. Even so, he admitted that the job sometimes takes a tremendous toll on his soul and his emotional health. But then he explained that three things in addition to his faith also helped to keep him from imploding:

1. **A positive focus**: He constantly reminds himself of the importance of the job he has been called upon to do by focusing on the lives he has helped to *save* rather than the tragedies he has been powerless to prevent.

2. **Support** : He credits his wife as the caretaker of his emotional health. His family in general and his wife in particular are constant sources of strength and renewal.

3. **Healing humor**: It's no surprise that humor is part of his self-care regimen, but he mentioned the movie *Dumb and Dumber* specifically. I'll admit this one took me a little aback. The idea that the preservation of one's emotional health could be in any way attributed to a Jim Carrey performance is so counterintuitive that it borders on the surreal. He explained that the broad comedy is so wonderfully meaningless and silly that it turns out to be the perfect antidote to the grim realities of his job. It's humor as therapy, and just what he needs.

Thankfully, there are people like this good man out there who serve all of us by being willing to look directly into the darkness of the human soul. The risks to his emotional and even physical health are very real. When we stare at monsters, they also look back at us and their poison can seep into our minds and hearts, destroying our ability to feel joy and hope, but the good doctor is wise and recognizes these threats. He first draws spiritual strength, but then he also takes positive steps to ward off the damage to his soul with three strategies that are wonderful tools even for those of us who don't have to toil in the basement of the human heart.

Keep the focus on the positive by constantly reminding yourself of your purpose and your triumphs. When I was a child, my mother provided the spiritual foundation that has sustained me all of my life. She loved the Psalms and told me many times that, although I was named after my father, David would likely have been her choice for a name anyway because he was her favorite biblical figure. David was a complex individual. A man of great faith and bravery, he was also vulnerable to very human temptations and at times fell into periods of deep depression.

The best-known story involving David is of course his victory over the Philistine giant, Goliath. When young David goes out to face what appears to be an impossible task, he reminds himself aloud of his past victories. In I Samuel 17:36 David says: "I have killed a lion and a bear and this Philistine shall be as one of these."

David was a shepherd boy still too young to be a soldier. He was only there in the Valley of Elah on an errand from his father to take some things to his older brothers who were in King Saul's army. All around him were battle-hardened warriors who knew how to fight and who probably had victories of their own to call to mind, but instead they looked at this gigantic brute bristling with sword and shield and sparkling body armor down in the valley and said, "look at the *size* of that guy!"

David, focused on his purpose and his faith and—remembering the lion and the bear against which he had already prevailed—marched down without as much as a sword or a helmet into the valley before the bellowing Goliath and felled him with a rock. Such is the power of faith and focus and the importance of calling to mind successes past.

Connect with others. Although David marched out to fight alone, the rest of us are perhaps not quite so spiritually fit or self-sufficient. We crave human contact as a basic need. We're social animals by nature and that innate need for contact has driven the communications revolution. Never in history have we been so readily connected to anyone anywhere on the planet. Wireless technology and the Internet have shortened the distance between any two people on Earth to a click of a mouse or the press of a button.

Paradoxically, the technology that brings us so close has also isolated us like never before. People don't talk in airports, they check their email on ever-present smartphones, tap away at their tablets, or shut out even the possibility of a conversation by overriding their sense of hearing with little white earbuds.

We used to have occasion to talk with people face-to-face in our daily activities. Not so very long ago people had daily occasions to interact with service people, delivery people and cashiers. We banked with actual tellers and on warm evenings we sat on the front porch where we talked with our neighbors. And when we watched television, it was one of three networks that about a third of the people we knew had probably also seen.

The arrival of the digital age has meant more convenience but far less personal contact with people outside of our Instagram contacts. Streaming and on-demand entertainment has allowed us to indulge our individual interests in ever-narrowing niches.

Now, given the chance to trade the convenience of ATMs, texting, and Skype for hand-written letters and a programming choice between a show about a talking horse or a show about a talking car, I think I'd take *now* over *then* every time. But every technological advance also has a cost, and the cost of specialized programming, the self-service checkout, and wireless technology has been an increase in personal isolation. The result is a crowded but micro-niched and lonely world. It's more important than ever to reach out to others, starting with the people closest to you.

Here's a disturbing fact about the price of increasing isolation and its effect on our families. In a typical modern family, eating dinner together is an increasingly rare event and, judging from a survey presented by the National Center on Addiction and Substance Abuse (CASA) that represents very real risk to our kids.

"The survey finds that the more often children have dinner with their parents, the less likely they are to smoke, drink or use illegal drugs," says CASA chairman and president, Joseph A. Califano, Jr. at Columbia University. "It is a tragedy that family dinners decline as teens get older."

Compared to kids who have dinner with their families twice a week or less, kids who eat with their families are a 24% less likely to try marijuana, a third less likely to smoke and about half as likely to drink. Why should eating together make such a difference? It doesn't have so much to do with the food as it does the seat at the table. In the time we eat without other distractions that isolate us, we have an opportunity to talk, to laugh and even to argue. We strengthen our connections to these people who share our address as we directly interact with them in close physical contact around the table for a few minutes each night nourishing our relationships just as we nourish our bodies.

Loving our spouses, our kids, and our parents isn't enough. Every connection we have requires ongoing maintenance. The support and strength we've nurtured will be tested. The time of crisis, when we desperately need the support from our loved ones, is a poor time to discover the consequences of failing to strengthen and reinforce family bonds.

The summer after my son was born, I went to our state fair. In the multi-purpose building, government agencies had set up information booths to educate the public about all the important things that they do. I stopped by the department of mental health booth. I don't remember why, maybe I was just checking to see if anyone was looking for me. Anyway, the woman at the booth asked me if I'd like to take a stress test. I said, "You mean like on a treadmill?"

"No," she explained patiently, "this is the department of *mental* health." I had apparently made it clear to her that an intelligence test wouldn't be necessary.

"Oh, sure," I said, "of course I'll take the test."

The test was something called the Holmes-Rahe scale. The Holmes-Rahe consists of a checklist of life-events that one has experienced within the past 24 months. Each one marked, like "divorce," "the death of a loved one," or a "change of residence," is assigned a certain number of "life crisis units". The more traumatic the event, the higher the number will be. The death of a spouse is 100 units, a job change is 36, and planning and taking a vacation is 12. When the units are tallied, the level of stress indicated by the score is a predictor of the likelihood of a stress-related illness in the coming year.

A score under 150 is considered healthy, 151-200 is mild and represents a 33% chance of illness, 201-299 is moderate and so the risk increases to 50%. At 300, the level is considered severe and the risk to health is about 80%. It just happened to be a very eventful year and when my score was tallied, it was something like 427.

"Oh my," she said when she looked at my printout. "That's very high."

Of course, learning my stress score didn't do much to alleviate it. Now I was stressed about how stressed I was. I thought I should tell the people close by to back up. I was one crisis unit from spontaneous combustion.

The woman could see I was alarmed and she said, "Now don't panic. I need to ask a couple of questions."

"You mean like is my insurance paid up?" I said.

"Like, do you have a job that you consider important?"

"Well, yeah, " I agreed. "I think it *is* important."

"Good," she said, "Now, do you have a supportive family?"

"Yes I do." I said. "I have a wonderful wife and a new baby and my mom, dad, and two sisters I love very much and they're all wonderful supporters."

"That's great," she said. "How about a group outside of family either at work, or church or somewhere that accepts you for who you are even when you fail?" Not "if" I fail, but "when"? How did she know? This woman was *good!*

I thought of friends and groups I was blessed to be connected with and confirmed that indeed I had such a group.

"Well then," she said, "Don't worry about your number."

"Don't *worry* about it?" I asked, incredulous, "But it's 427! I ought to have my initials on your machine as the high score!"

"Well, it is high," she admitted, "but the number is only half of it. You do something you believe in and you have support from family and friends. With that kind of support, I doubt there's a number you couldn't handle."

She was telling me that it was a question less of stress than of balance. The more stress, the more we need support and loving relationships to provide the counterweight to the crises that weigh on us, but for that support to be there, we need to be active. Play with your kids, eat with your teens, hug your wife or husband, call your mom, tell your friends how much they mean to you. Don't be afraid to *feel*. If you're a man forget those ridiculous macho notions you see in movies. It's not weakness to need love and support. We were designed for needing others, but we need to keep in mind that a need is not necessarily a right. Love like food, is best when it is shared, and seasoned with joy and shared laughter.

Guess what is the most bonding of all emotional experiences, the one that brings people together and most effectively breaks down barriers of race, religion, age, gender, and socio-economics? If you guessed "laughter" then you'd be, well, wrong. Shared laughter actually comes in second.

The number one experience to bond people is actually disaster.

Hurricane Sandy, 9/11, wildfires that have killed and displaced Americans were all terrible catastrophes, but they did bring out some of the best in people who opened their hearts, their wallets and some even their homes for the victims. But, for all of the good that it sparks in others, we really don't want to engineer disasters just so we can inspire generosity and human connection, so we'll settle for the next best thing. Laughter, when a group shares it, is a common emotional experience that erases boundaries and brings people together in a positive collective experience.

Over the past twenty years, companies have spent billions of dollars on team-building experiences for their employees to spend anywhere from a half day to a week at a time at retreats climbing ropes, rafting down fast moving rivers, or bruising office chair-shaped fannies in saddles atop temperamental horses.

I've presented at some of these outings and occasionally I've even participated. A couple of years ago, I was booked to present at a team-building retreat for a physician-recruitment company. It took place at a dude ranch in Michigan and I was invited to take part in the "survivor series" of planned team events. In the advance letter I was instructed to bring along my cowboy hat and boots and "clothing you won't mind soiling."

It sounded like fun. Having grown up watching westerns on TV, it was kind of a dream come true to ride and rope like my childhood heroes. As it turned out, though, as a cowboy I was more Billy Crystal than Ben Cartwright.

It started out well. I put on my western gear and I thought I looked pretty authentic except for the price tag I discovered still dangling from the back of my cowboy hat at the end of the first day. We rode horses along a trail that wound through a forest of tall pines. We ate steaks prepared chuck-wagon style, which meant well charred and on metal plates balanced on our knees. All along the gentle trail it was kind of a Roy Rogers experience, but when we got to the rodeo arena, it all went Rawhide.

The arena was about the size of a football field and surrounded by a tubular steel fence. It was covered with a deep loose mixture of sawdust and dirt and other "organic" material that finally explained why all cowboys wear boots. The entire area reeked of livestock. This was to be the site of our team-building survivor games.

We formed into teams and entered the ring for a few activities that included tug-of-war and a version of tag that required us to stomp balloons tied to the ankles of opposing team members. Then the ranch hands herded calves into the ring, each one with a ribbon tied to its tail. We chased the poor things around like Masai warriors on a lion hunt, yanking cattle-scented ribbons off their south ends with our bare hands (there's not enough Purell in the world to make that activity ok).

In the next part of the competition we broke into smaller groups for a variety of undignified activities like using verbal instructions to guide a blindfolded team member through an obstacle course that included barrels and piles of cow manure.

I didn't volunteer for that one, but I had to participate somewhere so when the activities leader said "chute dogging" and no one raised a hand, I half-heartedly lifted mine to signal that I was also a team player. Unfortunately, the leader saw me and said, "Ok, you!" Since I was the only volunteer, he drafted another *chute-dogger*, a woman in her forties with salon nails and perfectly coiffed hair. The only thing even remotely western about her outfit was the turquoise in her earrings.

We were led into one end of the ring by a wide gate outside of which stood a large horned bovine creature serenely chewing its cud, whatever that is. This animal was as high as my chest at his shoulder and although I'm no judge of livestock, I'd put his weight at about the equivalent of a full city bus. The guide gave us the goal. We were to work together to "dog" or wrestle down this powerful beast as he was driven with a slap on his rump from the chute. I was speechless. Cow wrestling? Why don't they call it by a term that I would have recognized before I volunteered like, "recreational trampling," or "suicide by beefsteak"? I've seen the crazies at the running of the bulls in Pamplona, but even they have the sense to run *away* from the horns.

I was supposed to grab this monster and muscle him to the ground. I remembered the letter had instructed me to wear clothes that I wouldn't mind soiling, but I had no idea they meant from the *inside*. I completely lost my David facing Goliath philosophy. I never killed a lion or a bear and the one visit I ever made to a farm I got chased by a duck.

I looked over at my partner and I could see immediately that she had no intention of breaking any of her freshly balanced nails, so there was no point in discussing strategy. I just pulled my hat down snugly and nodded my head to release the beast.

With a loud slap that raised a cloud of dust from his well-muscled backside, the steer bolted out of the gate and ran right by my partner who squealed girlishly and then for some unknown reason, slapped him again as he sped by. This additional giddy-up inspired the animal to an even higher gear and as he charged by I wrapped my arms around the horns and was immediately yanked off my feet so hard that my right foot popped out of my boot.

With a strength borne of pure undiluted terror, I hung on to the horns like Indiana Jones gripping the hood ornament on that Nazi truck. Amazingly, my hat stayed on but the brim flapped up like Prospector Pete. My lips skinned back from my clenched teeth and the whites of my eyes showed all around and—in the fierce wind produced by the hellish speed of the panicked animal—dried out so that I couldn't blink. Behind me I left stuttering tracks in the dirt from my remaining boot while my right sock fluttered like a flag of surrender.

Finally, physics overpowered adrenaline and my arms gave out. I lost my hold and—still unable to close my eyes or lips—plowed, face down, into the "nitrogen-rich" surface of the rodeo ring. I came up sputtering and rubbing my eyes looking like a coal miner but smelling like a used plumber's snake. When I got back to my cabin, I remember that it took a half hour to floss the rodeo ring out of my teeth.

Later, after the longest shower of my life, the whole group met for dinner and karaoke. Around the tables, everyone recounted the stumbles and comical pratfalls and yes, my short, terrifying ride and subsequent face-plant in the rodeo ring.

I don't know if there were any real team-building lessons from the tug-of-war, the ribbon chasing, or the chute-dogging. It doesn't matter. The real teambuilding took place later as everyone laughed at mutual embarrassments. Those moments of comedy were worth the trip and have become the bond that took a work team made of individuals and forged a unit built on a shared experience of joyful laughter. Falling face-first into fertilizer may not qualify as a disaster, but it's the next best thing.

Chapter 12
A Gift to Give Yourself

"To George Bailey, the richest man in town!"
-It's a Wonderful Life, 1946

L ike most families who celebrate Christmas, we have a few traditions that have become absolutely obligatory sometime after each Thanksgiving. On the trip to see the relatives who live in a suburb of Cleveland about 150 miles north of us, my wife drives while I read Charles Dickens' **A Christmas Carol**. On the way back I read the account of the first Christmas from the book of Luke. And on Christmas night we watch the 1946 Frank Capra classic, **It's a Wonderful Life**, with Jimmy Stewart and Donna Reed.

I've seen the movie often enough to serve as understudy for any character in the film from Uncle Billy to ZuZu. Somehow, when the whole town comes marching into the Bailey house one by one throwing into the fund to keep George out of jail, I get choked up. It's not the generosity of the characters or the relief that George isn't going to need to trade his gray flannel for black and white stripes. It's instead the look on George's face. His expression is one of complete and utter gratitude, the look of a man who has been given a second chance and knows how to appreciate it. It's a masterful piece of acting on the part of Jimmy Stewart and one of the classic scenes in the history of American film.

It also provides a great lesson for us on the gift of gratitude. If I were allowed to offer only one suggestion for experiencing more happiness in your life at home and at work, it would be this: adopt an attitude of gratitude.

Scriptures are packed with verses advocating praise as a worthy practice for believers in almost every book of both the Old and New Testament. I've heard cynics remark that for a deity, God sure seems insecure to need such constant praise but they miss the point. An all-powerful God would have absolutely no need of approval and praise. Praise isn't a gift we give, it's a gift we receive. What is praise but gratitude? A thankful heart is a happy heart. A thankful mind is peaceful. A thankful attitude is not only a pleasure to be around, it's literally a joy to experience because in it, our eyes are opened to what is good in our lives now.

Not long after my son was born, I developed an unusual illness in which I began to experience painful swelling in my joints, especially of the legs and ankles. I ran a low-grade fever for days on end and I lost energy. Every movement was a difficulty and before long I was reduced to shuffling like a man of one hundred.

My father had had a stroke in 1986, and for the rest of his life he walked slowly with two canes. I remember one evening at my parents' house I was walking down the hallway at the same time my father was working his way down from the opposite end. I felt his stare at the younger reflection of himself shambling in his direction. I caught his gaze and looked him in the eye, and then, with as much attitude as I could muster I growled, "Wanna race?"

The doctor ordered blood draws and tests. He ruled out rheumatic fever, Lyme disease, and lupus but he still had no explanation for the symptoms except that the blood tests indicated a high level of inflammation. Finally, he said that whatever it was, he was fairly sure it was stress related.

For the next month I was unable to run or to walk up the stairs without arthritically pulling myself along by the banister. Worst of all, I was unable to hold my infant son while I walked. I kept thinking of how effortlessly I had done all of those things just a few weeks before and how little I had thought to appreciate any of them. Now that I couldn't do the things that so recently had seemed unremarkable, they became the things I desired most in life. I imagined the exhilaration of charging up the stairs or running outside with the rushing wind roaring in my ears. Mostly, I thought most about walking with my new son in my arms. Every time I thought of that I felt desperate to get better quickly because the days seemed to be slipping by too quickly.

The condition and its exact cause were never diagnosed, but after six weeks or so, I began a steady improvement. The fevers lessened and my joints began to experience less swelling and more freedom of movement. Finally, I was able to do the things I'd dreamed about for weeks. I took the stairs two at a time, I ran to the store instead of strolling, and I walked for hours at a time with my child in my arms and a smile on my face. For a long time afterwards whenever I raced up the stairs of our home, I said a silent prayer of thanks that I could.

I would never again want to experience that kind of interruption in my health, but—like most trials—it had a lesson to enrich my life and make joy more available to me. The lesson was to pay grateful attention to the smallest things and to realize how blessed I am even when many things in my life are far from perfect.

It's an observable feature of human thought that the brain cannot experience two contradictory emotions at the exact same instant. When we say "mixed emotions" we don't really mean that we feel both happy and sad or hope and despair at the same time. What we do when we're in a conflicted emotional state is to switch back and forth between two or more perspectives. If we move from our old neighborhood to our dream house we feel happy and sad by turns. There's a moment of excitement and joy at the thought of the new experience before us followed by pangs of nostalgia at the thought of leaving old friends and the surroundings that have been the backdrop for so many good memories. We switch back and forth from joy to pain, but we don't really experience them both at once.

Just as joy and sorrow can alternate solos but can't do a duet, the same is true for gratitude and complaint. Complainers and cynics focus on imperfection and what, in their view, is lacking in their lives. But even the most pathological complainer can experience a change in outlook when he's forced to confront the possibility of losing the things he has so long taken for granted.

That was the story of George Bailey in that wonderful old Capra film. George has dreams of a life of adventure traveling the world. He has plans to travel and go to college and leave boring old Bedford Falls far behind. His plans change quickly when his father dies and there's no one else to take over at the Building and Loan. Enter Donna Reed and a depression and a world war and a snarling miser named Mr. Potter and George is facing middle age with a house full of kids and a cash shortfall that will likely send him to prison.

George wishes aloud that he had never been born, and—with the help of a guardian angel named Clarence—George gets the chance to see what that would have meant to the people he loves.

When the vision ends, nothing in George's external reality has changed. George still has a problem with the bank examiner, he still has more debts than income and he still has never left Bedford Falls. But a profound change has taken place *inside* George Bailey. He runs down the same main street of the same "crummy little town" to the same drafty house with the same loose newel post on the banister and he is suddenly the happiest man in the world. He even declares, "Isn't it wonderful? I'm going to jail!"

George learns to be grateful for all that he has and when he really regards his blessings, he doesn't just choose to stop complaining, he *can't* complain. His gratitude cancels out any negative perspective and the only emotion available to him is joy. He sees what until that moment has been invisible to him: his family, his home, his friends, and the knowledge that he has lived a life of purpose. If you would truly count your blessings from your family to the ability, if you are so blessed, to walk up your stairs, you might find yourself accurately described as George Bailey was, the richest person in town.

An attitude of praise and gratitude is neither magical nor delusional. It doesn't gloss over life's imperfections like an artist covering an inferior work with a new layer of paint. Instead it's more like a sculptor's chisel revealing the beauty that resides inside the stone by removing everything that obscures the final form. Complaining, bitterness, self-pity, anger, fear, and jealousy hide the loveliness in the living moment. Gratitude chips it all away until we can see the beauty that already exists in our lives. The key is recognizing the joy of this moment of living.

We've all heard the phrase, live each day as if it were your last, but we don't really like to think about our last day, so consequently, we don't strain ourselves to imagine it. But I have a little exercise that—with a little imagination—will teach a useful lesson in the power of gratitude for what you have right now. Instead of living today as if it were your last, try this: Live this day as if it were your *past*.

Here's your assignment. Imagine today that you're a time traveler. In reality it's now twenty years in the future but for some reason you've been allowed to return to this day in your life two decades before. Your family is before you as they were twenty years ago. Maybe your children are young adults again or maybe just toddlers. Your older loved ones are back again to talk to and to tell them the things you've regretted for years not having said. Your wife or your husband is younger again and—for today at least—so are you. Even the dog and the cat you remember so fondly are here. This is a miraculous second chance to live this one day in your life.

What would you do on a day like that? Would you give your family a distracted peck on the cheek on the way out the door, or would you wrap up your family in tight embraces and wonder why you didn't always pay such careful attention to fleeting moments of shared affection? Would your children's bickering and whining irritate you as it used to, or, in this visit to your past, would it suddenly sound like music in your ears?

When you take that future perspective today, you'll recognize the miracles that exist—as they always have—in the mundane. Little that frustrated and angered you two decades ago would find a toehold on that day. You might even find that the common pet peeves and irritants of work and family life not only became tolerable, they paradoxically became sources of absolute joy. How blessed you feel to have been given such a gift: a second once-in-a-lifetime with these irreplaceable people.

If you ask George Bailey or old Ebeneezer Scrooge, you might think that a second chance is perhaps the greatest gift anyone could ever experience, but maybe not. Maybe even better is living this day right the first time around and with the attitude of thanks that comes from discarding the unimportant and often trivial negatives that tend to anger and distract us from focusing on what really is important in this moment of living and what a joyous blessing it all is.

Chapter 13
Maintaining the Machinery

No discussion of emotional health would be complete without acknowledging the connection and critical importance of the physical. We know that the body and the mind are connected in a cybernetic loop relationship, but it's also worth pointing out how dependent our emotional health can be on the health of the body.

There are many individuals, like Barbara from the first chapter, who maintain their joy even when the body is seriously ill, but it's a monumental struggle because it's difficult to feel better emotionally than we do physically. A positive focus and a commitment to joy are much harder to maintain when we're suffering from the distraction of physical pain.

Likewise, when we're not fit physically, we're probably also not fulfilling our potential emotionally. If we want to give happiness and joy the greatest chance to be a reality in our lives, we need to take care of the instrument. That means putting the right things into our body and mind. It also means getting exercise.

Whenever I talk about exercise, I feel a twinge of guilt because exercise is number one on the list of things that are good for me but I don't enjoy like daily flossing and bran muffins. I've never been successful at any single exercise program, and I've tried quite a few. I remember one Christmas back in the 90's when my sister-in-law took a gift suggestion from my wife and bought me a "Buns of Steel" video. Now, there are certain things—bad breath remedies and anti-cellulite creams among the rest—that you should never buy another human being unless that person has specifically asked you to. For example, you don't want to receive an unsolicited personal trimmer unless you've made a public declaration that your heart's desire is less nose and ear hair.

Giving someone a Buns-of-Steel video is like that. I don't have much occasion to see myself from behind but apparently the view needs improvement. I popped the video in exactly once to see a man in leggings and an elastic headband chanting, "And *clench!* And *release.* And *clench!* And *release.*" and that! Was enough!

I think the whole "Buns of Steel" premise was a little ambitious anyway. The videos were most often purchased by people who had buns that looked like they were manufactured closer to Pillsbury than Pittsburgh. Promising steel in one video was a little optimistic, don't you think? Why not produce a progression of videos that would allow you to start slowly? You could work your way up to steel but first do, say, "Buns of Aluminum" and if you complete that, "Buns of Zinc."

They eventually produced a whole series of videos including, "Abs of Steel" and "Arms of Steel". I guess if you did them all you'd never get through another airport in your life. Every time through the metal detector it would be, *beep beep beep*, "It's my buns, officer. They're *steel*, you know."

As much as I dislike exercise I know it's necessary for physical health and an important component of my emotional health as well. I've tried many approaches, gadgets and expensive equipment. Unfortunately, most of them didn't last as long as the payments to own them did. My secret hope was that my body would see the Visa bill and just tone itself up, but that didn't happen.

I've bought balance balls, aerobic steppers, a punching bag (my Rocky phase), barbells, dumbbells, and an exercise bike for my wife that became an excellent sweater dryer. I think they should include that feature in the sales pitch. "It has a pulse meter, a custom-programmable course computer, and look how nicely your fine washables fit on those handlebars. I'm guessing that within three months, that's going to be the most important feature for you."

I bought a treadmill a few years back, because a walk is always so much better when it costs $800 and you don't end up anywhere. It came in a huge coffin-like box that I brought home and wrestled down the basement stairs. That was the only real exercise I got out of it. I put it together, tossing the instructions because, hey, I'm a man. When I was finished, I had only a few parts left over so I felt very proud of myself. I called my wife down to see the finished product. She eyed it suspiciously and asked, "Does it work?"

Insulted, I blustered, "Of course it works!" Then to prove it I plugged it in, climbed aboard and hit the 'on' switch. That's when I learned about the 'speed control dial'. It was twisted all the way to the right, a little practical joke from the guys at the factory, apparently. It turned my demonstration into a magic trick. I just hit the button and *vanished*! Consequently, I have cans of corn in my cabinet that have logged more miles on the supermarket checkout conveyor than I have on that treadmill.

The goal is to find the exercise approach that fits who you are and what you can sustain. Anything else is doomed to failure from the start. I'm thinking of my one foray into an athletic club where I went at the urging of a friend of mine. This friend lives in my neighborhood and is about my age. He's one of these guys who cuts his grass shirtless, but one of the rare ones who looks okay as he does it. There are two types of men, those who work in their yards in the summer without their shirts on and those who really shouldn't. Unfortunately, they're not mutually exclusive groups. I fall into the second category so I always wear a shirt when I'm outside, partly out of self-consciousness and partly out of consideration for the neighbors, but mostly out of fear of potential court orders.

Anyway, one day I was over at my friend's house while he was running the mower and I remarked, "You know, you really keep yourself in good shape. What do you do?" He said, "Dave, I do resistance training, I pump iron, I lift weights." Then he added this, "If you would go to the gym with me I could show you six simple exercises that would work all your major muscle groups and in *24 workout hours*, you could have a new body."

"Twenty-four hours?" I thought. "I could be buff by the weekend!" I learned later that 'workout hours' are something like dog years but in reverse. It means one hour a day, three days a week for eight weeks. Not what I was hoping for, but still I was game.

The next day I met him at his gym. He was wearing his Under Armor workout gear and carrying a thick leather belt to protect his back. I was wearing a campaign tee shirt from someone's failed bid for school board and white sweat pants with a pinkish tinge from being accidentally washed with a red sock.

We walked into the free weight area and up to a station with a bar on a stand set about chest high.

"This first exercise is one we call *squats*," he said, adding, "It's great for the quads, and the glutes."

I looked at him blankly.

"You know what those are?"

"Frat houses?"

"They're *muscles*!" he said, pointing to where they would be located on my frame if I did the squats. Then he placed the bar on my shoulders with some weight at either end and said, "Squat!"

This part of the exercise was pretty easy. All I had to do was allow gravity to take the bar in the direction it wanted to go anyway.

"Now come back up."

This was less easy, very painful and a little dishonest. The exercise was deceptively named after the easy part. To be fair they should be called "squat-and-come-back-ups. Regardless, I struggled through the pain and back to a standing position and shouted, "I did it!"

"Aw, that was one," he said. "I want you to do nine more for our first set and then I'm going to show you five more exercises of three sets each."

I did that math in my head and the answer came back, "This ain't going to happen today," but I said nothing. I kept on squatting and rising. After two or three more, with pain shooting down my legs and sweat dripping into my eyes I stopped and said, "Now remind me again, what is the benefit of this exercise? And don't tell me about 'quacks' and 'gloops'."

He said, "Dave, if you do this exercise for the next eight weeks, you're going to have a butt that can *crack walnuts*!"

"That's what we're working toward?" I asked. Then I put the weight down and said, "I don't *want* one!" Frankly, that's just not something I see myself using all that often. Not even as a party trick.

For me the exercise program that works best is the one that is just part of my day. I have an easy approach: don't ride when I can walk, don't walk when I can run. Simple choices like choosing stairs over a one or two floor elevator ride or a jog to the convenience store two blocks away rather than getting in the car can save gas and burn calories rather than the other way around. In the long run, we can reap real benefits from these little steps. Anything else is a bonus.

Could such a small and informal approach really make a difference? According to a 10-year study published in 2003, researchers concluded that a total of 7 minutes of stair-climbing every day (not all at once, but a *cumulative* 7 minutes) cut the risk of heart attack in men by half. I think the core of my fitness program is having a three-floor house and a bad memory. My office is in the attic and I'm up and down between the first floor and the top floor all day because I've left the phone in the kitchen while I'm at the computer in the attic and so I run down. Then I realize I've left my keys to the car on my desk and I'm back up. Downstairs again, I head for the front door and the post office a couple of miles away (otherwise I'd walk) and I see I'm not holding the envelope I needed to mail. Why? Oh yeah, I took it up with me when I went for my keys. The long-term result is a great heart but lousy knees.

Like all success habits, it's the consistency with which we do the little things that will produce results. I can join a club and then not go. I can buy expensive equipment and use it to block and dry my cardigans. Or, I can make the simple choice to deliberately park as far away from the handicapped spaces as my physical condition will permit. I can take the stairs rather than ride twenty vertical feet on the elevator. That's what works for me. For you perhaps the treadmill and the weights and the squats are what you need to maintain the equipment. If so, great! I salute you, but if you ever drop by with a bag of walnuts, bring your own nutcracker.

Chapter *14*
Playing with Pain

"To truly laugh, you must be able to take your pain, and play with it! -Charlie Chaplin

L ife is sometimes hard. I'll be the first to admit it. There are uncertainties and tragedies, victories and losses and never a guarantee that anything will turn out the way we've planned. Life bangs us up emotionally and physically. When you get right down to it, the enemy of happiness is either real pain or what we choose to interpret as pain. Actual pain is hard to deny whether it's the physical pain of illness or injury or the emotional pain of loss. The aim of this book was never to deny that authentic pain exists nor to suggest that we can or should be immune to it. It's instead to distinguish the difference between authentic pain and what we unnecessarily interpret as pain through poor perception and response choices.

Again, it all depends on what choices you make: What focus do you choose? How committed are you to experiencing happiness? How effectively do you minister to the needs of others? How healthy and compassionate is your sense of humor? What do you choose to take in? How consistently do you express gratitude? How well do you maintain the physical machinery?

Occasionally, someone misinterprets this message as an artificial shortcut to fool oneself into feeling happier rather than a guide for deliberate steps to experiencing genuine joy through faith, hope and love in action. That happened once when I was at a conference for school board members in northern Ohio. After the program, a man approached me and said, sneeringly, "Well, it must be nice to be *you*!"

I replied, "Well, it's not bad, but why do *you* think so?"

He said, "Well, I mean all this 'choose-joy' and 'change-your-focus' stuff is fine, I guess, but some people have some real problems and they can't just laugh it off."

I was unaccustomed to this kind of a response to the talk. Whether or not individuals are willing to commit to the message, I've found that the vast majority at least agree with the concepts. This was a new one for me.

He continued, "If you've found some way around pain, good for you, but that doesn't mean everybody is the same."

Here I had to stop him. "Wait a minute," I said. "Back up. Did you say I found a way *around* pain?"

"Well, yeah," he said. "It sounds like everything to you is just a big joke, but maybe some people have faced tougher things than you have."

"Wait a second," I said. "First, if that's the message that you heard, then I'm afraid I didn't communicate very well and I apologize for that because I've certainly never found a way around pain."

I related to him how I had experienced pain like everyone else. I have lost people I loved and I've seen people I care about suffer. I've been sick and I know what it is to feel desperately frightened and helpless while my beautiful son, at just 12 months old, underwent surgeries and chemotherapy. I've also known the unparalleled joy of seeing him come through that ordeal and grow up healthy and strong. In short, I know as much about pain as some people and less than others, but during no moments of authentic pain did I ever think it was just a joke.

On the other hand, I'm perhaps well enough acquainted with pain to know the difference between what is life and death and what isn't and I never want to get them confused. The really life and death painful moments have been real but thankfully rare. Most of life's painful moments are temporary and most could have been worse. You might have sprained an ankle, but avoided a break. You might have broken your leg, but you didn't need surgery. You might have required surgery but you didn't lose your limb. You might have lost a limb, but saved your life. It's a matter of what we're willing to consider and whether we choose to focus on our abundance or our lack that makes the difference in how we get through pain with our joy intact.

Just because I know the difference between real life-and-death pain and temporary pain doesn't mean that I'm happy with either experience, though. I've never welcomed pain however minor. If I could avoid it I would, but just because I don't enjoy it, that doesn't mean that I have nothing to gain from it. Every frustration, embarrassment, setback, sickness and minor injury has a lesson to teach if only we'll attend. There was a song we used to sing in Sunday school based on James Chapter 1, verse 2 that went: "Count it all joy when you fall into diverse temptations. Knowing this, that the trying of your faith worketh patience."

Because I have something to learn from my difficulties means that the trial could be good for me in the long run, but that doesn't mean that it feels too joyful in the moment of pain. In that moment I'm going to feel scared, angry, and hurt. When it's all over, though, I have a choice. I can enter that experience in the balance book of my memory as a liability, a negative confirmation that I am as cursed as I've always suspected. Or, with the right focus, determination, and sense of humor, I can count it all joy. It's an experience from which I can grow or maybe at which I can laugh. Maybe I can invite others to laugh, too and then the joy is multiplied. So, my intention is to choose joy. I want it to be my default mode for living. My challenge isn't to avoid pain, because that's impossible. My challenge is to get back to joy as quickly as I can.

I told that man a story that I think makes the point. I'm a dog lover and I always have been. While growing up, my family always owned dogs and some of my fondest memories include my dogs. Now I also love cats, so cat lovers don't need to email me demanding to know why I left them out. I have two cats at home and I love them. I think they love me, even though when I come home they sometimes run to their dishes first. After I've fed them they'll come up and rub against my ankles and I'll think, "There, see? They love me." Then they go do the same thing to the couch.

But the dog! The dog has a party every time I come home. I just open the door and say, "I'm home!" and the dog goes completely Tom-Cruise-on-Oprah on me. He's jumping on the couch, rolling on the floor, running in circles and making little sounds of unbridled joy at my arrival. I have to say I feel pretty good about that dog.

I have a friend whose wife has a little dog. This woman works outside the home so every evening when she comes home the dog has a little celebration just like my dog does for me. One night I was there visiting my friend when his wife came home. The dog went crazy and she started kissing the dog. Now I love my dog, but I'm not kissing my dog. You know why? Because I saw my dog give himself a bath. Ever since then we've had boundaries I just won't cross.

As this woman was kissing that dog, her husband leaned over and said, "She's happier to see the dog when she comes home than she is to see me."

I said, "Tell me the truth. When was the last time *you* licked her face when she came through the door? You have a party like that dog is having and she'll rub your belly, too!"

When my wife and I were first married we found a little dog and welcomed her into our home. She was an older dog, though, and after three happy years, she died. We were heartbroken, but soon we were thinking again about how nice it was to have a dog so we went to the animal shelter where we found a cute little 2 year-old female terrier with a scruffy face and big expressive eyes. We fell in love with her and started the adoption process. After the doggie social worker had asked us a lot of questions, she asked, "Now, what questions do *you* have?"

"Just one," I said. "Is she housebroken?"

She consulted her file and said, "Yes. The owners moved to an apartment building where they don't accept pets, but she is housebroken."

"Great!" I said, and we took her home. Within two weeks I learned something about our adoptee. She was housebroken, just not a fanatic about it. She would go outside to take care of business as long as it was convenient for her. In the morning she would come over to the bed and scratch at the blanket to let me know that she needed to go out. But there was no snooze button on the dog. If I wanted to roll over for ten more minutes, that was my choice, but when I woke up, there would be a little gift on the rug. The dog, completely unashamed, would be sitting by the spot with an expression like, "What'd I say?"

At that point I couldn't even get mad. It was true, she gave me the signal and I ignored it. It became clear that that dog was *training* me. You think you train your pets, but it's not true. They train you. Training is establishing or altering a behavior through teaching and reinforcement. My dog was a master of *negative* reinforcement. This dog should have worked in HR. I became so well trained that after awhile, I didn't even have to wake up to comply with the signal.

One dark cold winter morning at about 5 o'clock, my dog trotted over to the bed and gave one scratch at the covers. In a flash I bounded out of bed, bedclothes flying, I ran down the stairs, "Gotta let the dog out!" I mumbled, stumbling down the stairs with the dog in the lead. I hit the bottom and went charging through the living room heading for the kitchen and the back door.

I started to turn the corner toward the dining room and the kitchen beyond, but the TV stand had somehow been moved. Not much, but enough that it just wasn't where I expected it to be. I almost cleared it. Almost. I missed avoiding it completely by maybe a half inch, maybe less. I don't know because I've never actually measured the width of my little toe. That toe, of course was the only part that didn't miss that misplaced TV stand. It wasn't much, but it was enough.

I heard a snap, but for maybe five seconds I didn't feel any pain. There was some kind of delay going on while the nerve endings went into kind of a pitcher's wind-up. When the pain message finally arrived, it was indescribable. All I can tell you is that, until that moment, I had no idea I could speak Spanish. Suddenly I was fluent. My wife, who is a Spanish teacher, woke up and understood every word. "I believe he hurt his foot."

I would bet Mr. "Must-be-nice-to-be-you" would have given anything to be there that morning. He would have bought a ticket. Maybe he would have brought a bag of popcorn. And then, as I was rolling around in agony, he would have said, "Hey Dave, why don't you choose some *joy*? Oh, I know, how about you change your *focus*!"

I couldn't have done it. At that moment I doubt I could have told you my middle name because pain filled up my senses in ways that John Denver never wrote about. I didn't have a choice, I just had to respond to the searing, white hot pain in my pinky toe.

I remember how I once told this story to a group of seniors at a hospital in Ohio and a little woman came up to me afterward and asked, "What happened to the dog?"

I said, "I DON'T *KNOW*! I'm pretty sure you missed the point!"

Later, I went to the doctor. Have you ever been to the doctor for a broken toe? If not, see how long it takes to find someone who has. I promise it won't take you long to find one because: 1. People are clumsy, and 2. The toe is one of the most baffling designs in nature. Think about it for a second, we have big meaty pads swinging at the end of two long, double-hinged sets of bones, and on the leading edge of all this pendulum motion are five fragile, nerve-packed piggies. Didn't someone in quality control see a problem with that arrangement?

"So these are the schematics for the feet?"

"Yes."

"Um, what are these five little extrusions on the front?"

"Oh, those are toes."

"Toes?"

"Yes, they provide balance and stability."

"Oh no, no, no. One TV stand in the dark and those are going to snap right off. No, lose the toes and slap on a couple of impact-resistant bumpers."

If you've found someone who has seen a doctor for a broken toe, ask him or her what the doctor did. Chances are the answer was, "He taped the broken toe to the good toe beside it." That's the correct answer and it's basically, well, *nothing*! It's called "buddy-taping" but it should really be called "the easiest day in medical school." It doesn't even sound medical. Buddy-taping? Really? That's not a term for medical procedure, that's a camp activity.

My doctor did an X-ray (because he had to bill for something) and then came back a few minutes later with a big film of my foot; He popped it up on the light board and said, "Oh, that's *broken*."

I said, "Yes, well, I thought the toenail on the *bottom* was a bad sign."

Then I asked, "What are you going to *do* about it?" And that's when he got out the tape and taped the broken toe together with its unbroken neighbor like some quick fix from Home Improvement and said, "There you go."

I looked at the tape. "That's it?" I said.

"Unfortunately," he told me, "there's very little we can do for a broken toe of this nature."

Irritated, I asked him, "Well what if I'd lopped the toe off? Would you have a procedure *then*?"

"YES!" he enthused, apparently missing the sarcasm. "If you preserve the digit," –no kidding, that's what he called it— "we could reattach it. Why, you'd probably get full use back!"

At first I was amazed and then I thought, "What is 'full use' of a little toe?" The only use my little toe has ever demonstrated is the ability to spread wide enough from the other four to remove sock lint. I couldn't imagine going through surgery and months of therapy just to regain that ability.

I asked the doctor, "What if I needed a new heart, and there were a donor available? Aren't there surgeons who can put a new heart in my chest?"

"Sure," he said. "Major organ transplants are almost routine."

"Ah," I said, "But you're telling me that if I *stub* my toe, medical science is *baffled*?"

He thought about it for a moment and then answered, "Well, yeah, that's about the size of it." Then he added, "I mean I can't put a cast on it. It's too small. " Then grinning, he added, "No one could sign it, what good would that do you?"

True enough. So here's the question: Where does anything we've talked about in these pages have to do with this situation that was very painful, but—since I've never heard of 'death by severe stubbing'—probably not life and death? Was it in the moment that it happened? Not for me. In that moment I had pain and very little choice but to respond to it. Was it in the hours following? Again, I was in pain and not feeling particularly mirthful. Maybe someday I'll get to be just that good at these choices, but I'm not there yet.

For me, it was in the next four or five weeks, when I was stumping around like Captain Ahab that I began to have some choices. I could point to my inconvenient ouchie and say, "Well, this is typical!" In other words, I could have framed the experience as a pessimist, explaining my injured digit as a product of my bad luck and proof that God just doesn't seem to like me all that much. Thankfully, I wasn't raised that way. I enjoyed the blessing of being raised in a family that placed a high premium on humor, especially when it was directed at oneself. My dad was known for his stories of his own embarrassments and misadventures and no one enjoyed his stories more than he did. My two sisters are naturally funnier than I ever hope to be and my mother has the best sense of humor of anyone I've ever met. So when I got home from the doctor with my duct tape therapy from Dr. Red Green, I called to tell her.

Now, I wasn't really looking for her humor. I wanted understanding. I wanted maternal sympathy. In other words, I wanted mommy to kiss the boo-boo. So I dialed her number and when she answered I said, "Mom, guess what I did," and told her about my injury and she said, "Oh honey, I'm *so sorry* . . . HA HA HA HA HA!" Gee, thanks, Mom. But, you know what? I started to laugh, too. For the first time I began to really see the humor potential in the pain.

Soon I was telling the story to other people and they were laughing as well. It got better (the story, not my toe). People I worked with asked me to tell them the story. I told it and they would laugh. It was fun.

Have you ever had a great story to tell? It makes you very popular. If I was around someone who hadn't yet heard the story, I would emphasize the limp until they asked, "What happened to your foot?" (Showtime!)

"Sit down! I'll tell you about it."

Like Charlie Chaplin's advice, stories about stubbed toes and stumbles and embarrassments are really just ways of playing with our pain. I was playing with my pain and the payoff was the laughter of others as I told it.

Think about that for a moment and then answer a question. If I could go back in time to that morning and I could have known then what a great response I'd get from the story and all the laughter and the attention I'd enjoy by telling it over and over to so many people, yet this time I had the *choice* to avoid that TV stand, would I?

The answer is: YES!!! Are you kidding me? Were you really thinking I might do it on purpose? "Well, it *was* a pretty good story." No! I don't care how much laughter I enjoyed later, I would never willingly choose pain. I'd step around it and then make up a story. What are you going to do, ask for a note from my doctor?

But here's the thing: We don't *choose* pain. Pain chooses us. Loss, injury, illness, grief, frustration, anger. They all choose us. My choice would always be to avoid pain, but—because I'm not given the choice—pain is inevitable. My choice will be: "What I do with it once it's here?"

Your choice isn't whether or not you'll have pain. You will. You will have physical pain. You will have periods of emotional distress. You will have spiritual valleys when God Himself seems far away. That's not pessimism, that's life. It goes with the journey. Your choice isn't whether you'll have pain. Your choice is whether you allow the pain to render you helpless.

Your choice isn't whether you'll have grief. As long as you risk loving another person in this life, sometimes you'll lose who and what you cherish most. Your choice isn't whether or not you'll have grief; your choice is whether you allow your grief to make you hopeless.

Your choice isn't even whether or not you'll be angry. As long as there is injustice and unfairness in this imperfect world, there will be frustration with situations and with those other people you work with and live with whose priorities are not always identical to your own. You can be sure that sometimes you're going to get angry. Your choice isn't whether or not you'll be angry; your choice is whether or not you allow that anger to make you a cynic.

Your happiness, your level of stress and your ability to cope with change and conflict and pain of every type is—thank God—not solely a matter of what happens to you, but what you choose in response to it. The bad news is that, as long as you live, you will occasionally have pain. The good news is that, with the right choices, pain doesn't have to have you.

Chapter 15
Writing on the Wall

One of the greatest writers and perhaps the greatest American humorist was Samuel Langhorne Clemens, a.k.a. Mark Twain. His stories and essays are national treasures and all reveal a fierce intelligence and a rapier wit that hasn't been diminished by over a century since his death. Twain was irreverent in his humor. He never minded poking fun at power and he never apologized for refusing to bow before the altar of public opinion. His first published book was **The Innocents Abroad** (1869), a collection of essays about his travels through Europe and the Holy Land aboard a side-wheel steamer called the Quaker City.

America was a young country less than one hundred years removed from its status as a colony of the British Empire. Most of Europe regarded Americans as backward and lacking sophistication and because of this, most Americans felt a deep inferiority to all things European. As a result, European art and culture was held in a kind of reverential awe. If any

American was fortunate enough to visit Europe, he was expected to exclaim over the majesty of the art and the refinement of the culture.

Mark Twain was not any American, however. When he came to the old world, he did so with an attitude that refused to be dazzled by anything he saw. When guides showed him great works of art by Michelangelo, he pretended he'd never heard of him. They showed him a document written by Christopher Columbus and he dismissed it as a poor example of penmanship. They showed him the Holy city of Jerusalem and he declared that it needed a coat of paint.

His determination to drive his hosts (and not a few American editors and readers) crazy with his deliberate refusal to be impressed is as hilarious now as it was then. In most of the pages of the book, Twain is deliberately unfazed by almost everything he sees. But in France, he visits the Castle D'If, where he toured the damp prison dungeon where for over 200 years, political prisoners were confined to serve out their sentences, which were almost invariably for life. As Twain walks through the dank empty cells of this subterranean man-made hell on earth, he is genuinely moved by the names carved on the walls. As he describes the cells, the great humorist makes no attempt at humor. Twain is clearly deeply moved by the evidence of such human suffering and the pathetic attempts made by these absent souls to quite literally make their mark on the dark forgotten corner of the world in which they lived:

> *How thick the names were! And their long-departed owners seemed to throng the gloomy cells and corridors with their phantom shapes. We loitered through dungeon after dungeon, away down into the living rock below the level of the sea, it seemed. Names everywhere!--some plebeian, some noble, some even princely. Plebeian, prince, and noble had one solicitude in common--they would not be forgotten! They could suffer solitude, inactivity, and the horrors of a silence that no sound ever*

disturbed, but they could not bear the thought of being utterly forgotten by the world. Hence the carved names.

When I meet people who are just miserable human beings, bereft of faith or hope or joy, I sometimes wonder at what force keeps them imprisoned in their despair. For some, their lives have been scarred by tragedy, and my heart and my prayers go out to them. For some it is genuine clinical depression that is an illness no more a choice than to be diabetic and they, of course, need compassion and treatment.

For many, though, it's just a feature of their personalities to be habitually gloomy and joyless. It seems such a hard life and it would seem to me that the possibility of adjusting my behavior in ways that could bring me closer to moments of happiness would be worth any chance of success, however slim. Yet, some are absolutely dogged in their misery, just as if they were imprisoned. Then I think back on Mark Twain's walk through the tragic dungeons of that old castle, and I think I understand.

Misery and unhappiness are the by-products of fear. The pessimist constantly fears the worst possible outcome. For him, the future is filled not with bright possibility but with treacherous and as yet unseen hazard. So dreadful is that future, that the present becomes unbearable. The response to that fear is a cynicism and negativity that becomes not just what he feels, but who he is.

What is universally the greatest fear? No matter what you've heard, it's not dying and it's not speaking in public. I've been a stand-up comic, so I should know; I've sometimes faced both at once. It's instead the *loss of identity*. We can lose everything in this world, as those prisoners in the depths of that castle did, and we will still carve our names into the walls because we cannot bear the thought of being "utterly forgotten" as if we had never existed.

The cynical pessimist has forged his identity out of his negativity. With every expression of gloom, every prediction of disaster, every opinion of hopelessness, he carves his name into the walls of a prison he has built himself out of the unyielding rock of his bleak beliefs. He may understand that it doesn't have to be so. He may know the way out requires only some new response choices to break out of his prison, but to do so would be to repudiate everything he's ever said and done. It's tantamount to losing his identity, a fear even worse than living in the scarred dungeon of his misery. So he stays and toils away, making it a monument to his own self-inflicted suffering and desolation.

Hence the carved names.

My favorite feature on Facebook is one that allows me to send a brief message to any friend in my network and when I do, they receive a message that says, "Dave wrote on your wall." In a way, everything we say and do in our life is like that. Our words and our actions are a mark we leave on the world and in the hearts and minds of the people with whom we come in contact. Some are light impressions and others are carved deeply into the memories of others for reasons good or ill. The impressions we make with our joy and compassion and out of an attitude of service and love are like fine art, while those that are inflicted with anger and selfishness are like spiritual vandalism. Neither is easily erased.

It's inevitable that we each will leave our mark on the world. Whether we carve our names into the dead stone of our own dungeons of self-pity or in the treasured memories of our children and our fellow human beings is a choice we make every day. When we live in this moment with faith, with hope, with love and with joy, how can we make anything that isn't lovely?

Long before I began speaking for a living, I was a high school teacher of English and speech. I loved the job. I think the call to teaching is in the DNA. I taught, my wife was a teacher, my sister was a teacher, and even my wife's sister is a teacher. In both of our families, it's genetic. I was more successful some days than others, but I always knew that what I did mattered. I know that because now, many years after I graded my last essay, I still hear from former students who tell me how they enjoyed my class or that they learned something that came back to them when they needed it. There aren't many professions that can still affirm your efforts years later in the way that teaching can. I loved it and I have the highest respect and admiration for those who do it.

When I interviewed for my first teaching position, I had just graduated from college. I'd been on several interviews and I began telling people only half-jokingly that the typical interview went something like: "Can you teach? Can you coach? Answer the second question first." In what was at the time a tight job market, it became clear that the schools were interested in the value-added talents one brought to the table. I desperately wanted a job. Consequently, I was willing to agree to almost anything. Could I coach football? Sure. I could coach anything, that is unless winning was a priority.

Even though I agreed that I could coach anything from synchronized swimming to skydiving, every administrator I interviewed with seemed to know that I just wasn't coaching material, probably because most of them were. Do you think it's an accident that most school administrators are men and that so many of them look like Bill Belichick?

At one point in the interview, I was asked if I thought I could direct the school plays. Now here was something that I really felt that I could do. I'd been a high school thespian myself and had always had an interest in acting. So eventually I became the high school drama director in a school that had no budget for plays.

In the old building where I taught, the stage had doubled as a gymnasium before a new addition was added in the mid 60's. A lot of older buildings have a set-up where the gym is also the auditorium with a small proscenium at one end for concerts and awards programs. This was the only school building I've ever seen where a dedicated auditorium with fixed theater-style seats faced a huge stage area with a gym floor. There remained basketball hoops at either end of the stage area and all the court markings on the floor. It must have been interesting to play basketball on a court where charging out of bounds would mean doing a half-gainer into the orchestra pit, but that's how it was.

At the top of the balcony was a small, unheated room that had originally been used as a projection booth. The only view of the stage was via two tiny openings with counterweighted sliding panels to allow the projector lens to poke through. This was our control booth for the lighting person who had to watch and listen for lighting cues through a six-inch square and over the ominous hum of the antique light board that looked and sounded like something from Frankenstein's lab and filled the little room with the smell of ozone.

The walls of the booth were painted an industrial green and almost every square inch had been covered in what I first took to be typical graffiti, but on closer inspection turned out to be an unofficial archive of the history of the drama program. Here was the name of the young man who played Captain Fisby from **Teahouse of the August Moon**. Near the door was a short poem from a cast member of **The Time Machine** to his director, Mrs. Murray. By the time I arrived, the names of the actors and the shows in which they had appeared covered a span of twenty-five years. Before long, the casts of my own plays would be inscribed there as well.

For our first production, though, we would have had trouble scraping together seventy-five cents for the Sharpie to write a name. We had no money for costumes, for scenery or for printing tickets or programs. We also had no money for scripts or for the royalties to perform the show. The only solution was to create a play and scrounge whatever we could for props and set-building material.

I was presented with a script that the previous drama teacher had written in college called *The Voice of the North: A Melodrama In One Act*. I took the script and reworked it and what I ended up with was a live-action equivalent of a Dudley Do-Right cartoon complete with a heroic Canadian Mountie, a mustachioed villain and a damsel in distress named Sweet

Gardenia Dookin. The script had many flaws, but excessive subtlety wasn't one of them.

The casting required a tall, strong, square-jawed type to play the hero, named Honest Harold. At the tryouts I met Joe, a 6'2" senior who was built like a linebacker but with a gentleness that was sincere and endearing. He was, I thought, a perfect choice for my hero. I remember calling for him during rehearsals, "Where's my hero? I need my hero!" Joe's face would redden as he shuffled onstage.

For the villain I needed someone extroverted and willing to be over the top. The actor who did the best job of portraying the villain's gleeful wickedness was, coincidentally, Joe's little brother, Tony. Having drawn the protagonist and antagonist from the same litter, I completed my in-bred cast by giving the role of the female lead to Joe's real-life girlfriend, Kelli.

With the casting done, I turned my attention to the set design. I wanted to be as minimal as possible with just a few boards here and there to suggest the interior of a cabin. The only piece that required a degree of building ability was a moose head that was to be mounted over a cardboard fireplace. Since there was no wall, the head had to be free standing. Using brown felt, chicken wire and scrap lumber from the industrial arts classes, I set about making a head that turned out to be bigger, heavier and more dangerous than any actual moose's. It had an antler spread of seven feet and rocked unsteadily two and a half yards above an inadequate base.

With my casting done and the moose-scraper constructed, we were all set. The cast did a great job and before long the day arrived for the in-school performance. It was chaos. Students filled every seat in the auditorium as I rushed around shouting orders to the cast and crew. Every few minutes a tech crew member would charge in and announce another crisis: a light was out on center stage, the deed was missing from the prop table, Joe only thought to bring white socks to wear with his already too short uniform. There was no end to the situations.

In the midst of all the madness, Tony asked me to help him with his mustache. We'd just gotten together enough money from the ticket sales to buy a few things we needed for the performance. One of those things was a mustache for the villain. Now that we had it, it needed to be trimmed to fit Tony's upper lip. Every few minutes he would tap me on the shoulder and ask if I could trim it for him.

"In a minute!" I'd say each time just as the stage manager would slide through the door like Cosmo Kramer with news of the latest disaster. After maybe a half dozen requests to do a little barbering, I said, "Okay, okay, sit down."

Snatching up a long pair of shears I used for cutting construction paper, I snapped them twice along the lower edge of the synthetic facial hair. On the second cut I encountered some resistance but muscled through. It was at that moment that Tony did a move straight out of a Tex Avery cartoon. His eyes bulged like a frog caught under a radial and he produced a high-pitched whistling noise that wasn't loud to me but might have shattered my eardrums if I'd been a Chihuahua. In my tonsorial haste, I had caught a small piece of his upper lip between the blades of the shears and clipped it off along with the whiskers.

Tony began to bleed. I shouted for someone to fetch the school nurse. Now this was in the days before educators had in-services with titles like "Blood-borne Pathogens and You" so while we waited for the nurse to arrive I was without sterile gauze and latex gloves to cope with the gore. Instead I just held my jacket sleeve to Tony's mouth to stanch the flow.

Finally, the nurse walked in with a well-supplied first-aid kit and an air of reassuring calm that contrasted dramatically with my wild-eyed panic and bloody sleeves. As she slipped on a pair of blue examination gloves, she surveyed the desktop that now looked like a site of ritual sacrifice and remarked, "You know the mouth is a very vascular area."

Really.

As she went to work on Tony with ice and surgical sponges and creams, I told the stage manager to inform the office that we'd need to cancel the show.

"No, wait, Mr. Caperton," Tony said through a mouthful of gauze and cotton, "I think it's slowing down."

I said, "I think you're running out."

"No, no," he insisted, "I think I'll be okay."

I looked at the nurse who shrugged her shoulders as if to say, "It's your call."

Satisfied that the blood flow had indeed slowed almost to stopping, we supplied Tony with a large bandana that he stuffed into the pocket of his jacket and on he went. What a trouper! He was amazing. He would deliver his line and blot. It was inspiring.

The next day we were to take the show to the elementary school. The props were minimal except for the enormous moose head on its spindly stand. It took three people to muscle the moose through the doors and to the curb where a truck was to come to load it for transport to the elementary building. We lined up along the curb to wait for the truck. Big Joe stood beside the moose and it dwarfed his large frame. He craned his neck to the left to see if he could spot the truck. Behind him the moose swayed in the April gusts. We soon learned the aerodynamic weaknesses inherent in my design.

The moose had a wide rack of antlers that acted as sails in the strong breeze. In one rogue gust the giant head did a lazy half roll and listed beyond its tipping point. It fell like a giant redwood, throwing an ominous moose-shaped shadow over Joe just before it swatted him to the sidewalk. Tony, his lip swollen to twice its size, helped me lift the fallen moose from Joe, whose right arm had taken the brunt of Bullwinkle and an angry purple swelling was rapidly forming at the point of impact.

We helped Joe to his feet while he assured me that it was nothing and that he would be fine to perform. I thought, "I'm wiping out the entire family."

Throughout the show, Joe's arm hung uselessly at his side like a five-pound salami while Tony couldn't pronounce any lines with "P's" or "B's" in them. I was clearly going to be the subject of a lawsuit and there was still one last show to get through.

That night was the community performance and both my main male characters were bloodied and bruised. I knew that their mother would be coming that night, so I resolved to take the coward's way out and wait in the booth above the balcony after the show until the crowd had left the building.

That night, the kids did an amazing job. Their timing was wonderful. Joe was comically heroic, Tony was gleefully villainous, and Kelli added just the right touch of saccharine sweetness as the imperiled Gardenia. I was so enthusiastic about their performance and all they had overcome that I forgot my cowardly plan and rushed down to the stage to congratulate them. As I was passing out my compliments, a voice spoke up behind me and froze me in place.

"Mr. Caperton? Could I talk to you for a minute?"

I turned to face Joe and Tony's mother, a smile plastered unconvincingly across my sweating face.

"Oh, Mrs. K, hi!" I said, "Of course you can."

I braced myself for a tongue-lashing or the promise of litigation, so it was a surprise when she said, "I just wanted to *thank* you."

I looked behind me to see if someone had appeared over my left shoulder who hadn't maimed her two boys.

"*Thank* me?"

"Oh yes," she said smiling broadly, "I always knew my boys were talented, but I had no idea how funny they were." She seemed genuinely moved and her expression was equal parts pride and gratitude. "*You* brought that out of them."

I was so relieved that she didn't want to discuss legal action that I was almost giddy. "Oh don't be silly," I babbled, "Really, thank *you!* Hey, they're great kids. Listen, I've still got *pieces* of them!"

There were many shows after that one, each one with its own disasters and crises, although thankfully none was ever again as bloody as that first. After the final performance of that show, the first cast of my era of drama students wrote their names and the names of their characters on the walls of the control booth. Many of those inscriptions were addressed to me, "*Hi Mr. Caperton, remember me, signed Kelli, a.k.a. Sweet Gardenia, the Voice of the North,*" "*To our director, Mr. C. We love you, the cast of Our Town, 1994.*" Over the next ten years, names I recognized took their place alongside the decades of names I never knew.

It was just two years after that first show that I got the call that every teacher hopes to never receive, but almost all eventually do. It was Kelli and her voice was strained and hoarse. "Did you hear about Joe?" she asked.

"No," I answered as I felt a chilling dread.

She explained that there had been a fire at the apartment building where Joe had been living. It had broken out in the middle of the night and everyone had gotten out safely. But there was a two year-old girl living there as well and, although she'd been evacuated, Joe didn't see her and so assumed that she was still inside the building. He rushed back and kicked in a door.

The inside of the building had become a vision of hell. The superheated air now topped 800 degrees and when Joe kicked open the door it rushed out and struck him like a molten fist, searing his lungs and stopping his heart. They said he was gone before he fell.

My hero.

Years later, the day finally came to move on. I packed boxes of books and keepsakes and stacks of pictures signed by students and placed them carefully in the trunk of my car. But not all of my mementos could go with me. The building was empty of people by the time I had everything packed away, but I had one more thing to do before I left.

I walked up the stairs to the dim balcony of the auditorium and I let myself into the lighting booth. For the next hour or so I read all those names on the walls, names that belonged to young men and women who had come through this room on their way to life and some, like Joe and two others whose names I read there, to untimely death. And I thought, "What a *privilege* I've had to do this job. What a shame it would have been if I'd done it without joy."

What about you? What about the lives you touch each day at work and at home? Are you accomplishing your mission with joy? Are you communicating that joy to others? Are you finding happiness?

The level of happiness experienced in your life is determined partly by what happens to you, but mostly by how you respond to it. It comes down to choosing what you will do. Will you define your success by the stuff you can buy or by the joy you create? Will you choose a focus that allows you to recognize the privilege in what others around you might even describe as pain? Will you habitually express gratitude for the miracle of every moment and for God's grace to allow you to fulfill your purpose for one more day? Will you eliminate anger and fear and instead choose to take in the kinds of thoughts and images that will give you strength when the pressure is on? Will you consistently communicate joy to those around you with something as simple as a Duchenne smile? And will you use compassionate healing humor to distinguish between what is really life and death and what is just a stubbed toe ?

Life is a gift too precious to waste in misery and unhappiness or questing for gain that in the end will mean nothing. At the end of this life, your amassed wealth will be of no more value than brass and all of your fame and power you'll learn was a vain illusion. Instead, you'll tally how much of God's gift of joy you experienced for yourself by how much you created for others.

Now it's up to you. It's your name on that wall and however you choose to write it, remember, it's going to be there for a long, long time. You know how-to and hopefully now you've also been reminded why-to. So make your choice, and make your mark.

And, oh yes, smile.

About the Author

Dave Caperton, "The Joy Strategist," is an international speaker and author on the power of a joyful mindset to beat stress while increasing engagement, unleashing creativity, strengthening health, super-charging learning, and providing legendary service and outstanding care. He has been an educator, a performance consultant, a stand-up comedian and comedy writer and has given over 700 keynote presentations to top organizations in business, education and healthcare.

For more information about booking or interviewing:

Email Dave at: **dave@davecaperton.com**
URL: www.davecaperton.com
Phone: 740-JOY-FULY